Teachers' Unions and Interest Group Politics

Teachers' Unions and Interest Group Politics

a study in the behaviour of organised teachers in England and Wales

R. D. Coates
Lecturer in Politics, University of York

Cambridge
At the University Press
1972

Published by the Syndics of the Cambridge University Press
Bentley House, 200 Euston Road, London NW1 2DB
American Branch: 32 East 57th Street, New York, N.Y. 10022

© Cambridge University Press 1972

Library of Congress Catalogue Card Number: 72-83595

ISBN 0 521 08739 2 Hard covers
0 521 09752 5 Paperback

Printed in Great Britain by
Western Printing Services Ltd
Bristol

Contents

	Preface	*page* vii
	Glossary of educational terms and abbreviations	xi
1	Teachers and their Associations	1
2	Traditional Forms of Teacher Pressure	8
3	The Limits of Traditional Pressure	20
4	Relationships of Power and the Changing Context of Bargaining	34
5	Organisational Unity and Professional Self-government	47
6	Militancy	61
7	The Alliance for Educational Advance	81
8	The Alliance with Organised Labour	94
9	The Determinants of Interest Group Behaviour	112
	Bibliography	130
	Index	135

Preface

This is a study in the behaviour of a particular set of interest groups, the teachers' associations of England and Wales; and unlike the majority of interest group studies before it, it is concerned with the *behaviour* of organised groups rather than with their *influence*. Explanations of group behaviour must analyse both the choice of power-centre to be pressured (interest group *strategy*) and the means adopted to pressure the centre chosen (interest group *tactics*). The strategies and tactics of the teachers' associations of England and Wales are our concern here.

The study attempts to meet two needs. Primarily, it fills a major gap in our knowledge of the detailed working of British Government in the 1960s. For though many studies exist of the National Union of Teachers as an educational interest group, the vast majority of them draw on material that is at least a decade old; and all of them suffer seriously from a lack of systematic reference to the parallel activity of the other associations, from whose impact the N.U.T. is never totally free. For though the character of teacher politics in England and Wales cannot be understood without a detailed consideration of the N.U.T., studies of the N.U.T. alone cannot adequately describe teacher politics that embrace at least seven other major associations of teachers. Not since 1915 – and Beatrice Webb – has a serious attempt been made to describe and explain the strategies and tactics adopted by all the major teachers' associations; and the marked change in those strategies and tactics in the 1960s makes the need for a systematic reconsideration all the more pressing.

By concentrating on the *behaviour* of teachers' associations, the study also attempts to clarify a central confusion in many studies of interest group politics – namely their tendency to run together questions of 'behaviour' and 'influence'. Not since H. Eckstein's *Pressure Group Politics* was published in 1960 has any systematic attempt been made by political scientists to locate the determinants of what he called the 'form' of pressure group activity. In the last chapter, the argument will return to this theme, to specify the determinants of the behaviour of organised teachers in terms applicable to the behaviour of interest groups outside the education sector.

The organisation of the study reflects the argument within it. Traditionally, the teachers' associations have relied on a limited and unchanging set of strategies and tactics in their attempt to shape the policies of governments; and these are considered in Chapter 2. Their strengths and inherent weaknesses are drawn out through two case-studies in Chapter 3. Yet all is not traditional in current teacher politics. Since 1947, and particularly in the 1960s, the relationships of power within which organised teachers bargain, and which conditioned the strategies and tactics that they traditionally adopted, have changed markedly. To the degree to which this was recognised, the teachers' associations altered their behaviour. Chapter 4 discusses this changing context of power, and Chapters 5–8 describe and evaluate the teachers' associations four-fold response to it: their search for professional self-government, their militancy, their alliance for educational progress, and their search for an alliance with organised labour. The final chapter considers the more general question of the determinants of interest group behaviour.

Many people have given time and expertise in the writing of this study, and I would particularly like to thank the senior officials of the eight teachers' associations and of the Association of Education Committees, without whose co-operation it could never have been completed: Sir William Alexander, H. E. Birkbeck, R. J. Cook, T. Driver, Sir Ronald Gould, F. Jarvis, Geraldine Jones, M. G. Powell-Davies, K. Ronald, J. H. Smith, Miss L. Spalding and Miss S. Wood. I would like to thank those who supervised or commented upon the work at its various stages: George Bain, D. N. Chester, Allan Flanders, Jean Floud and W. J. McCarthy; and also A. H. Halsey and W. J. M. Mackenzie, who examined the doctorate thesis from which this book derives. The Warden and Fellows of Nuffield College, Oxford, provided shelter and sustenance for long periods of the research; and of late, the study has benefited enormously from the comments of three colleagues at the University of York – Lawry Freedman, T. V. Sathyamurthy and Gerald Studdert-Kennedy. In recording my gratitude to them all, I of course absolve them, individually and collectively, from any responsibility for the final outcome. That responsibility, for better or worse, is mine alone. The only other people at whose feet praise or blame can be laid are

Dorothy, Emma and Ben, who between them have lived with the teachers' unions for longer than they would probably care to remember. To them, and to the memory of a great friend, teacher and trade unionist, Haydn Morgan, the book is dedicated.

Glossary of educational terms and abbreviations

A.A.M. The Association of Assistant Mistresses.
A.E.C. The Association of Education Committees.
A.M.A. The Assistant Masters' Association.
A.M.A., The The Journal of the Assistant Masters' Association.
A.M.C. The Association of Municipal Corporations.
A.T.T.I. The Association of Teachers in Technical Institutions.
Authorities' Panel, The The employers' side of the Burnham Committee, 1920–65.
Board of Education, The The Government Department responsible for education, 1902–44.
Burnham Committees, The The committees in which teachers' salaries are negotiated, between representatives of the Government and the local education authorities on the one side and of the major teachers' associations on the other. The Main Committee settles the salaries of teachers in primary and secondary schools; whilst other committees (formally autonomous, but in practice subordinate to the Main Committee) settle the salaries of teachers in further education.
C.C.A. The County Councils' Association.
C.E.A. The Council for Educational Advance.
Central Advisory Councils Committees created by the 1944 Education Act to produce in-depth reports on major educational topics; from which have come studies on primary education (the Plowden Report), on the education of the child of average intellectual ability (the Newsom Report), and the recent report on teacher training (the James Report) amongst others.
C.F.E. The 1963 Campaign For Education.
Circulars Advisory and informational documents issued by the Department of Education and Science.
Code, The The highly detailed and mandatory regulations laid down by the Department of Education for elementary schools in the fifty years after 1870, which defined standards, curricula, teacher qualifications, building requirements and so on.
Comprehensive schools Non-selective secondary schools, taking children from the full range of educational ability.
C.O.P.P.S.O. The Conference of Professional and Public Service Organisations.
Department of Education, The The Government Department responsible for education in the last quarter of the nineteenth century.
Department of Education and Science, The The Government Department responsible for education since 1964.

D.E.S. The Department of Education and Science.
Direct Grant Grammar Schools Semi-independent secondary schools with a selective intake.
Elementary schools Schools taking children from ages 5 to 14. The vast majority of schools between 1870 and 1944 were of this kind; until they were replaced in the wake of the 1944 Education Act by primary and secondary schools.
Further education Education provided in separate institutions for students over the statutory school-leaving age.
General Secretary The senior full-time official of each of the teachers' associations.
G.N.P. Gross National Product.
H.M.A. The Headmasters' Association.
Head Teachers' Review, The The Journal of the National Association of Head Teachers.
Higher education A term often synonymous with 'further education', but also used to designate the university and college of education (teacher training) institutions.
Joint Four The four associations of secondary school teachers: the A.A.M., the A.M.A., the H.M.A. and the Association of Head Mistresses. The four share a common headquarters, normally pool their respective resources, and hold regular joint meetings.
Local education authorities The bodies statutorily empowered to provide educational institutions (universities apart), and to employ teachers.
Lord President of the Council, The The political head of the Department of Education before 1902.
L.E.A. Local Education Authority.
Management Panel, The The employers' side of the Burnham Committee since 1965.
Minister of Education, The The political head of the Government Department responsible for education, 1944–64.
Ministry of Education, The The Government Department responsible for education, 1944–64.
Minister of State, The The junior Minister at the Department of Education and Science.
N.A.H.T. The National Association of Head Teachers.
N.A.L.G.O. The National Association of Local Government Officers.
N.A.S. The National Association of Schoolmasters.
New Schoolmaster, The The Journal of the National Association of Schoolmasters.
N.F.P.W. The National Federation of Professional Workers (the white-collar affiliate of the T.U.C.).
N.U.T. The National Union of Teachers.
Permanent Secretary, The The senior civil servant in the Government Department responsible for education.
President of the Board of Education, The The political head of the Government Department responsible for Education, 1902–44.
Primary schools Schools taking children up to age 11.

Primary-secondary differential, The The lower salaries that, on average, teachers in primary schools receive relative to their equivalents in secondary schools. This differential arises, in part, because of a concentration of highly paid teaching posts in secondary schools.

Regulations Statutory Instruments drawn up by the Department of Education and Science and its predecessors, laying down mandatory requirements on the local education authorities.

Review, The The Journal of the Headmasters' Association.

School Boards The bodies responsible for the provision of elementary education 1870–1902.

Schoolmaster and Woman Teachers' Chronicle, The The title of the weekly newspaper of the National Union of Teachers until 1962.

Secondary schools Schools providing education for children aged 12–19.

Secretary of State for Education and Science, The The political head of the Department of Education and Science.

Selective secondary schools (or grammar schools) Schools taking only those children who – via examinations and school reports – are deemed at age 11 to be the most 'intellectually able'.

Teacher, The The weekly paper of the National Union of Teachers, 1963–.

Teachers' General Council The instrument of professional self-government sought by the teachers' associations in the 1960s.

Teachers' Panel, The The employees' side of the Burnham Committee, on which sit representatives of the main teachers' associations recruiting amongst the teachers covered by the Committee.

T.U.C. The Trades Union Congress.

1

Teachers and their Associations

School teachers are amongst the most highly organised of English workers, and the associations that recruit them are amongst the oldest of interest groups and the earliest of white collar unions. There are now in the region of 400,000 teachers employed in the schools and institutions of further education in England and Wales, three of whom in every four belong to one or more of the eight major unions that negotiate on their behalf: the National Union of Teachers (N.U.T.), the Joint Four Secondary Associations,[1] the National Association of Schoolmasters (N.A.S.), the National Association of Head Teachers (N.A.H.T.), and the Association of Teachers in Technical Institutions (A.T.T.I.).

The teaching profession as we know it was a product of the educational expansion of the last quarter of the nineteenth century; and the associations that currently represent it were, in the main, created in this period of tension and change. Embryonic unions of elementary teachers had formed earlier, and the prestigious Headmasters' Conference first met in 1869; but the major associations of elementary and secondary teachers did not emerge until educational expansion (and with it, the growth and status of teaching as a profession) became a major issue in British politics – that is, in the period initiated by Forster's Education Act of 1870.

From its emergence, the teaching profession was internally divided, and the existence of so many major unions bears witness both to the former fierceness of those divisions, and to their continued relevance for teacher politics. As the number of teachers grew after 1870, they organised themselves into associations largely in competition with one another, so giving organisational expression to rivalries and hostilities that continue to bedevil them. In particular, Victorian middle-class secondary school teachers organised themselves into what are now the Joint Four Secondary Associations, to defend their status and privileges against the rapidly expanding

---

[1] The Assistant Masters' Association (A.M.A.), the Association of Assistant Mistresses (A.A.M.), the Association of Head Mistresses, and the Headmasters' Association (H.M.A.).

body of elementary teachers, already organised from 1870 in the National Union of (Elementary) Teachers. Equally, the hostility between class and head teachers within the elementary teaching force generated separate organisations of both within the N.U.T., of which the National Association of Head Teachers remains; and a similar tension between class and head teachers (and indeed between men and women teachers) in the traditional secondary schools explains the formation of not one but *four* secondary associations in the last quarter of the nineteenth century. The current fragmentation of teachers' unions was then completed by the formation of the A.T.T.I. in 1904, and by the breakaway from the N.U.T. of men hostile to its policy of equal pay, a breakaway which culminated in the formation of the N.A.S. in 1922.

These divisions within the profession, though now less intense, remain; and indeed have in part been sustained by the policies of the very associations whose separate existence is predicated on their continuing relevance. Historically, the organisational rivalry of the teachers' associations has made its own contribution to the creation of a profession in which levels of earnings, career prospects, and status are in general greater for men teachers than for women, for graduates than for non-graduates, for head teachers than for class teachers, and for teachers in institutions of further and secondary education than for those in primary schools. Both as a cause and as a consequence of this, teachers in general continue to work alongside those with similar qualifications and of a similar sex. So primary teaching remains the preserve of the non-graduate female teacher, whilst teaching in selective secondary schools is dominated by graduates, and that in institutions of further education is largely in the hands of men. It is this clustering of teachers by sex, qualifications and type of school, and the different earning, career and status prospects that they experience, which continues to be the basis on which eight separate teachers' associations can be sustained.[2]

THE TEACHERS' ASSOCIATIONS

By far the largest of all the teachers' associations is the National

[2] These trends have been intensified by the rapid growth of the teaching labour force since 1947. The size of the profession has doubled in the last twenty-five years, a growth largely concentrated in secondary schools and in institutions of further education.

Union of Teachers, which currently has at least 225,000 serving teachers in its membership. Alone of the eight associations, the N.U.T. recruits amongst all qualified teachers, and yet significantly, two-thirds of its members are women, and in 1960, over a half taught in primary schools. Indeed, the Union was then the only association recruiting women teachers in the primary sector in which they predominate. Even amongst secondary teachers, the N.U.T. recruits mainly outside the grammar schools. Again in 1960, though a quarter of its membership taught in non-selective secondary schools, less than 6% taught in either state or direct grant grammar schools.

The N.U.T.'s major competitor for the support of men teachers is the National Association of Schoolmasters. This union has grown rapidly since the war, and is now the second largest association with a membership in 1967 of 40,000. Two-thirds of these teach in secondary schools, again mainly concentrated outside the grammar school sector. The major union recruiting men teachers there remains the Assistant Masters' Association which, as the largest of the Joint Four, had 26,000 serving teachers in its membership in 1967. At least 80% of these were graduates. Of comparable size, but with many fewer graduates, is the A.T.T.I., whose 25,000 serving members in 1967 worked almost entirely in institutions of further and higher education.

The other associations are smaller. The A.A.M. had 18,000 women teachers in its membership in 1967, the majority of whom – as with the A.M.A. – were graduates working in grammar schools or (in areas where schools had been reorganised) in schools with six forms, as the mistresses teaching at sixth-form level. Head teachers, on the other hand, either remain in the N.U.T. or N.A.S., or face a choice of three associations. Head teachers in primary schools – the majority of whom are women – normally join the N.A.H.T., 80% of whose 1,500 members in 1967 were heads of such schools. Heads of state and direct grant grammar schools, on the other hand, tend to join the much smaller Headmasters' Association, or the Association of Head Mistresses, both of whom had less than 2,000 members in 1967.

The pattern of growth within the teaching labour force since the war has strengthened the basis of the sectional organisations within the profession. Growth has come primarily in those educational institutions where male teachers predominate, and where the smaller

associations recruit most. The major casualty of this has been the
N.U.T. It is clear from Table 1 that as late as 1950, two-thirds
of all teachers belonged to the Union. That figure is now no higher
than one teacher in two. More specifically, with the growing membership of the three other associations recruiting male class teachers
– the N.A.S., the A.T.T.I., and the A.M.A. – the N.U.T. no longer
unionises a majority of men teachers. In fact an absolute majority
of teachers in further education, nearly a majority of head teachers,
and probably 80% of all graduate teachers in secondary schools
now belong to other associations. Where the N.U.T. has maintained
its strength is amongst *unionised* women teachers, nearly 90% of
whom remain in the Union.

Table 1. *The changing distribution of serving teachers between the associations*

	Total* %	N.U.T. %	N.A.S. %	Jt.4 %	A.T.T.I. %	N.A.H.T. %
All serving teachers						
1950	81	64	5	10	2	4
1967	75	50	9	10	6	3
All male teachers						
1950	91	60	13	15	4	3
1967	87	40	21	15	12	3
All female teachers						
1950	75	67		7	0.4	4
1967	66	57		7	1.0	4

* The discrepancy between the total figure and the sum of the associations on each line is due to the incidence of joint membership.

This changing distribution of membership is the fuel which feeds
the continuing tensions and competition between the teachers'
associations themselves. This tension is least between the N.U.T.
and the A.T.T.I., who ended competitive recruitment by a settlement in 1941. It is greatest between the N.U.T. and the N.A.S.,
between whom there has been a long and acrimonious struggle for
the allegiance of the growing number of men teachers. More
generally, the heavy reliance of each association on only particular
groupings within the teaching labour force has reinforced the ten-

dencies endemic in all similar but distinct organisations to emphasise policy differences, to accentuate sectional differences amongst their actual and potential memberships, and to seek to monopolise the loyalty of groups so sectionalised. This struggle to hold and to attract members and the sectionalism to which the associations give expression and support, colours the whole set of relationships that make up teacher politics – politics which at national level focus around negotiations with the Department of Education and Science and with the national associations of local education authorities.

THE SYSTEM OF EDUCATIONAL ADMINISTRATION

It is impossible to understand fully the strategies and tactics adopted by the teachers' associations without reference to the structure of government within which the associations seek influence. Universities apart, state educational institutions are provided, and teachers employed, by local education authorities in England and Wales. At national level, these local authorities belong to three associations: to the Association of Education Committees (the A.E.C.), and to either the Association of Municipal Corporations (the A.M.C.) or to the County Councils Association (the C.C.A.). These national associations represent the local authorities in their collective dealings with the Department of Education and Science, and act as 'employers' in national negotiations with the teachers' associations – a role they share with the D.E.S. itself.

For local authorities provide schools, and employ teachers, under the 'control and direction'[3] of the Secretary of State for Education and Science.[4] Yet this is not a highly centralised system of administration. The Department has no powers to actually build schools or to employ teachers. Nor are the local authorities merely the agents of the Central Department. In the day to day running of the education system, power lies at local level, and the Department's role has traditionally been that of adjudication and control. True, it

[3] Education Act 1944, 7 & 8 Geo. 6, ch. 31, section 1(1).
[4] Before 1964, the Secretary of State was known as the Minister of Education, and before 1944, as the President of the Board of Education. Similary, the Department of Education and Science was the Ministry of Education before 1964, and the Board of Education before 1944. In the text, current titles will be used unless specific reference is being made to earlier periods.

possesses a number of general controls over the activities of local education authorities, but these controls have rarely been used this century to dictate the detail of educational content. Instead they have been used to control the magnitude of resources consumed, and to enforce minimum standards of educational provision.[5] The Department's general reluctance this century to control educational content and teaching methods has left day to day control of the education process in the hands of the local education authorities and their teachers.

Moreover, the Department has long been willing to involve the national associations of local authorities in consultations and negotiations on issues affecting local education authorities generally. It does this formally, through the set of permanent advisory committees mainly set up by or since the 1944 Education Act, and through working parties created to consider particular issues; and it does so informally through regular contacts between the permanent officials of the Department and those of the local authority associations. This departmental willingness to discuss proposed policy with outside bodies extends to the teachers' associations, and the resulting pattern of consultation is habitually referred to as the educational 'partnership'. By it,

> The content and wording of Regulations are always the subject of discussion – often prolonged – between (the Secretary of State), the local education authorities, the teachers' associations and any other body concerned. So far as it is possible, Regulations are, by the time they are published, agreed documents...While it is not so vital to obtain unanimous agreement about the terms of Circulars, since these are not mandatory documents, the (Secretary of State) will, as a rule, consult a wide range of opinion before issuing one on an important matter of national policy . . . and it is possible for weeks, or even months, of consultation and negotiation to take place before an important Circular reaches its final form.[6]

---

[5] The most recent exception to this general rule is the use made by both Labour and Conservative Secretaries of State of their controls over the building programme to advance or to stem secondary reorganisation.

[6] H. C. Dent, *The Educational System of England and Wales* (London, University of London Press, 1966), pp. 73–4.

For although there is a high degree of local autonomy in the detailed administration of the education system, a number of forces have combined to increase the importance of national decision-making. The Department's insistence on the maintenance of national minimum standards, the teachers' associations' own search for support against recalcitrant local authorities, and the very existence of national associations of L.E.A.s and of teachers have been centralising agencies; and in consequence a whole range of issues that affect serving teachers are now determined at national level, to apply to all local education authorities. Teachers' salaries are negotiated nationally in the Burnham Committees.[7] Their contracts of employment normally follow the model drawn up by the A.E.C. and the teachers' associations. The conditions within which they work are immediately affected by Departmental Regulations on class size, on teacher training and qualifications, on the rate and form of school building, on the school leaving age, on secondary reorganisation and the question of selection, even by the lack of national policy on the detail of educational content; and thus, ultimately, by national policy on the size and growth of educational expenditure. It is to influence these issues that the teachers' associations adopt the forms of behaviour that are the subject of the chapters that follow.

[7] For a detailed study of these Committees, see R. D. Coates, 'The teachers' associations and the restructuring of Burnham', in the *British Journal of Educational Studies* (June 1972, pp. 192–204).

2
Traditional Forms of Teacher Pressure

Since the last quarter of the nineteenth century, teacher pressure has taken one of three forms. In their search for influence at national level, all the associations have developed direct and regular contacts with the permanent officials and political heads of the D.E.S. and of its predecessors. On occasions, all have supplemented this direct pressure by the lobbying of M.P.s; and each, to varying degrees, has established contacts with the mass media in an attempt to win public support for teachers' demands. Because these forms of behaviour alone are both long established and common to all the associations, they can be said to constitute 'the traditional forms of teacher pressure'.

RELATIONS WITH THE DEPARTMENT

Access to the Department

The lobbying of the Education Department by associations of teachers is as old as the systematic involvement of the State in the education sector. As early as 1852, a deputation was sent from the Metropolitan Church Schoolmasters' Association to oppose the education policy of Lord Derby's Government, and a year later, Lord Granville received a deputation representing the church school teachers of England and Wales.[1] The attitude of the Department to this early activity of elementary teachers varied with Permanent Secretaries and with Ministers. The 'kindly' reception given by Granville in 1853 compared favourably with that of Robert Lowe, a decade later, that 'teachers desiring to criticise the Code were as impertinent as chickens wishing to decide the kind of sauce in which they would be served'.[2] From its formation in 1870, the

---

[1] See A. Tropp, *The School Teachers* (London, Heinemann, 1957), p. 49.
[2] D. Thompson, *Professional Solidarity Among the Teachers of England* (New York, Columbia University Press, 1927), p. 76. The 'Code' was the body of administrative regulations laid down by the Education Department.

N.U.T. regularly sent deputations and memoranda to the Department; and Sir George Kekewich later described the hostility with which these were met in the 1880s.

> The National Union . . . was not 'recognised', and the Department pretended to ignore its very existence. The officials were forbidden to correspond with the secretary of the Union, and if he brought forward any complaint on behalf of a teacher, he was actually told to refer it through the managers of his school, and no further notice was taken of his letter.[3]

It was only in the 1890s, with Kekewich as Permanent Secretary, that the N.U.T. first established regular and informal contacts with Departmental officials. Relations between the Union and his successor, Sir Robert Morant, were more formal and cool; and not until he was replaced in 1911 were present relationships finally established, with Departmental officials receiving and seeking Union reaction and opinion on all aspects of educational policy at an early stage in its formulation.

Unlike the N.U.T., the Headmasters' Conference and the H.M.A. experienced no initial hostility from Departmental officials. From their foundation, each enjoyed 'easy access to them in unofficial and informal ways' because their leading members 'belonged to the same social class as the Cabinet Ministers, the Chief Permanent Officials, and the majority of Members of Parliament, and had, in fact, often been their tutors and headmasters'.[4] As the Headmaster of Eton told the 1914 Headmasters' Conference, the absence of 'public utterances' by the Conference was not indicative of a lack of influence, as it might have been in the case of the N.U.T. Rather, 'they were able to bring a great deal of influence to bear on those in authority in a very quiet way'.[5]

This degree of informal and regular access to Departmental officials was denied longest to the N.A.S. Before 1944, to have an audience with the President of the Board, or after 1944 the Minister,

[3] Sir G. Kekewich, *The Education Department and After* (London, Constable, 1920), p. 62.
[4] Beatrice Webb, *English Teachers and their Professional Organisation* (a special supplement to the *New Statesman*, vol. 5, no. 129, 25 September 1915, p. 21).
[5] G. Baron (unpublished Ph.D. (Education) thesis, University of London, 1952), p. 400.

was a rare event, achieved after lengthy preparation and much lobbying. Even in the 1950s, many doors remained closed and information from the Ministry given out to the other associations was not given to the N.A.S. The significance of the Association's entry to the Burnham Committee in 1961 lay here, in gaining for it full consultative status.

The changing nature of the relationship

The Headmasters' Conference apart, the earliest contacts between the Department and the teachers' associations were both formal and irregular. The associations gathered what influence they could through occasional deputations to the political heads of the Department, and through their more regular submission of detailed memoranda. This use of deputations and memoranda continues; but the role of such formal contacts has altered, and their significance as channels of influence has waned. They are no longer the sole, or even the major technique of pressure. The associations now bring their influence to bear on the policy-making process by their membership of advisory committees, and by regular and informal contacts between their permanent officials and those of the Department.

The committees are basically of two kinds: *ad hoc* working parties and permanent advisory committees. On complex issues, where the associations' policies are both detailed and divergent, the establishment of a Departmental working party (on which the associations are directly represented) is a common stage in the generation of legislation and in the revision of administrative regulations. On such working parties, protracted negotiations occur within terms of reference laid down in preliminary discussions at the Department. For example, a conference of representatives of the teachers' associations, the local authorities and the Department in 1963 set up a working party, on whose later recommendation the Schools Council for the Curriculum and Examinations was established. In 1967, the N.U.T.'s sanctions campaign ended in the creation of three working parties, on all of which the major teachers' associations were represented.

In addition, the Department is surrounded by a network of permanent advisory committees, whose composition is not always so closely tied to the structure of the teachers' associations. To the Burnham Committees that negotiate teachers' salaries, and to the

Schools Council, the associations have rights of direct nomination. To the Central Advisory Councils, they, in common with a large number of educational pressure groups, can only submit written and oral evidence. The Burnham Committee and the Schools Council are major channels for association pressure on issues central to their memberships; and the N.U.T., for example, recently used the Central Advisory Council's 'Plowden Report' as the basis for a major campaign.

Pressure through committees of this kind is supplemented by a high degree of personal contact between officials of the teachers' associations and of the Department. Routine issues and individual cases are the subject of day-to-day contact by telephone, letter or in person between association officials and the personnel of the relevant Departmental branch. The initiative for this informal contact does not come solely from the associations. The Department seeks their views on a wide range of issues. A constant stream of draft Circulars, and requests for opinion, advice – even, at times, assistance – finds its way from the Department to the associations; and Departmental officials on occasions visit the associations' headquarters to discuss proposed policy.

Within this pattern of informal and regular contact, the functions and significance of deputations and memoranda have changed. Once the sole source of access to the Department for the N.U.T. and N.A.S. at least, deputations have now come to serve, in part, a public function: to indicate difficulties of negotiation on particular issues or to assure the associations' memberships that in a sensitive area consultation is in fact taking place.[6] But they do not only have this public function. They are also a means of maintaining pressure on the Department when informal contacts fail. The Joint Four experience may be taken as typical.

Whenever the Department asks for the Joint Four's reaction to a proposed Regulation or Circular, the Secondary Associations normally consider the matter separately. They then produce memoranda, which are often amalgamated into a joint submission. But if the Regulation or Circular raises matters of particular importance to the Associations, or if it contains proposals which they cannot accept, these memoranda will be followed by a joint deputation to the relevant branch of the D.E.S., or to the Secretary of State himself;

[6] On this, see R. A. Manzer, *Teachers and Politics* (Manchester, Manchester University Press, 1970), p. 11.

and perhaps as many as twelve such deputations will be organised, on average, in any one year. For example, in 1969 Joint Four deputations saw the Minister of State on the position of head teachers under the Race Relations Act, and saw the Secretary of State on his attitude to sixth-form colleges. Earlier deputations discussed with Ministers, amongst other things, the problems of secondary reorganisation, school buildings and the training of teachers.

When interviewed, officials of the associations testified to the willingness of Departmental personnel to consult them on proposed policy initiatives, and to the openness of both permanent officials and political heads to their requests for meetings. Each stressed the importance of informal over formal means of contact as a source of influence; one said, the associations are 'always listened to and always consulted'. This consultation during the formulation of Departmental policy is the major channel through which all the associations bring their pressure to bear; and the personal contacts, committee-work, deputations and memoranda that it requires are the major tactics adopted by each. Their additional reliance on Parliamentary pressure and the mobilisation of public opinion are secondary forms of behaviour (in which not all participate to the same degree), whose purpose ultimately is to affect the terms of reference within which that consultation with the Department takes place.

RELATIONS WITH PARLIAMENT

The lobbying of M.P.s has long been seen as legitimate by associations of teachers employed within a sector dominated by Government. As early as 1887 the N.U.T. conference rejected a sole reliance on pressure on the administration, arguing that 'the teachers had gone too often to the Education Department and too seldom to the Department's masters'.[7] Many associations were established with this form of pressure in view. The Headmasters' Conference was created to defend the privileged endowed schools against the intrusion of the State, and the H.M.A. was formed to give those excluded from the Conference influence in the reorganisation of secondary education thought imminent after 1889. The formation of the A.M.A. followed the absence of evidence from assistant masters to Select Committees of the House of Commons in the 1880s. As

[7] D. Thompson, op. cit. p. 169.

the N.U.(E.)T. President told its first conference, 'there was no class of men whose daily duties and personal interests were more frequently interfered with by legislation, and hence the teachers must by necessity unite to influence such legislation'.[8]

When Beatrice Webb described the behaviour of the associations in 1915, she documented the primacy of what she termed 'teachers' politics'. The N.U.T., she wrote

> . . . had carried to a high point all the methods of political agitation; by agitation in constituencies it had brought pressure to bear on individual candidates and M.P.s; by constant deputations to the Education Department, questions in the House and energetic lobbying it exercised influence on Permanent Officials and Cabinet Ministers. It had secured several hundred representatives on Local Authorities, educational and otherwise; and two Members of Parliament, one a Liberal and the other a Unionist.[9]

As contacts with the Education Department developed, the primacy of Parliamentary pressure waned. But since major amendments to the working conditions of teachers still require legislation, Parliament remains a key area of association activity; and the failure of pressure on the Department invariably moves the associations to Westminster. As recently as 1962, the N.U.T. created a Parliamentary Committee to hold a watching brief on Parliamentary legislation or incipient legislation affecting teachers or teachers' interests, to prepare draft amendments to Parliamentary Bills or proposed Bills and to maintain contact with the Union – supported M.P.s. Its creation only regularised the present practice of the Union where Parliamentary affairs are concerned.

Local pressure

The associations learnt the importance of local contacts early. Tropp

---

[8] A. Tropp, op. cit. p. 110.

[9] B. Webb, op. cit. p. 21. Mrs Webb included as part of 'teachers politics' relations with the Department that are here considered as a separate form of behaviour. It is significant that in 1915 these should have appeared as secondary to, and in support of, pressure aimed primarily at Parliament. For a similar conclusion on the primacy of Parliamentary pressure for the N.U.T. before 1914, see D. Thompson, op. cit. p. 168.

wrote of the 1870s that 'deputations of schoolmasters . . . waited on (M.P.s) almost every time they visited their constituencies'.[10] And a century later the N.U.T. salary campaign of 1967 still began with deputations of teachers to local M.P.s; and local pressure was a key element in the N.A.S.'s abortive campaign for a Royal Commission on teachers' pay in 1965. Even associations who rarely lobby nationally – like the N.A.H.T. and Joint Four – often urge their local branches to approach M.P.s in their constituencies. The A.M.A. made such an appeal in its salary campaign of 1954, as did all the Joint Four Associations in their demand for an interim pay award in 1969; and the H.M.A., in their pension campaign of 1962 asked members to approach M.P.s either by direct action or through local Joint Fours.

Every local association of the N.U.T. has its own Parliamentary Correspondent. The Union attaches great importance to his work of establishing wider and more permanent contacts with M.P.s. An executive circular in 1960 urged local associations to invite the local M.P. to functions, to address their meetings, and to meet them after each Union conference; on the principle that keeping M.P.s informed of local teachers' problems and of their attitude to educational developments, and of the work of the Union at local level, could be of considerable value in stimulating Parliamentary support.

Such local activity is at its height at General Elections; and the form of behaviour adopted here has changed little since the last quarter of the nineteenth century. The N.U.T. made use of elections from its formation. Tropp described the process.

> At the 1880 and 1885 elections, the local associations were requested by the executive to organise deputations to all parliamentary candidates. In 1888 steps were taken to strengthen and consolidate the influence of the Union. A complete register was formed of the constituencies within the district of each local association, of their representatives in Parliament, and of 'prominent politicians' who were interested in educational matters. These 'prominent politicians' were sent information on educational matters, and it was hoped that they would act as a further pressure on M.P.s and prospective M.P.s. In 1890, 'Parliamentary Regis-

[10] A. Tropp, op. cit. p. 139.

ters' were prepared in which every promise made by a Member of Parliament was registered for further reference.[11]

Each election is taken as an opportunity to inform candidates of association policy. The A.M.A. in 1950, and in subsequent elections, sent guidelines to local branches on how best to approach Parliamentary candidates, and for what purpose. At each post-war election, the N.U.T. has drawn up lists of questions to be put to candidates by Parliamentary Correspondents; and the N.A.S. normally issued a policy statement which local associations can use to formulate their own questionnaire.

Lobbying at national level

The associations regularly sent letters, pamphlets, and memoranda to M.P.s, and have on occasions organised petitions. The N.U.T. first adopted this approach as long ago as its pension campaign of 1875, when a statement of Union policy was forwarded to Members of both Houses. Almost a century later, the same tactics were still in use. The Joint Four, A.T.T.I. and N.U.T. organised a petition in 1961 against Ministerial intervention in the Burnham Committee. The N.A.S. circulated a petition in 1969 in support of an independent inquiry into teachers' pay. It is more common for the four Secondary Associations to send joint letters; but individual associations have written to M.P.s when an issue sufficiently aroused them. The N.A.H.T. circulated a salary memorandum to M.P.s in 1966, and the N.U.T. that year wrote to all Members arguing that the teachers should escape the worst rigours of the incomes restraint.

The associations have made regular use of private meetings with groups of M.P.s and especially with Party Committees. As early as 1871, the N.U.(E.)T. held a meeting with a group of M.P.s on teacher reaction to the Code, which led to a deputation of M.P.s and teachers to the Minister. Nearly a century later (in 1966) the question of compulsion in school meal duties was discussed first between the President of the N.U.T. and a group of M.P.s who were Union members, and later with the Home Policy Committee of the Labour Party Executive. In their campaign for access to the Burnham Committee, the N.A.S. met 55 backbench Conservatives in 1950, the 'Conservative Education Group' in 1952, and in 1957 both the Conservative

[11] A. Tropp, op. cit. p. 140.

Party Education Committee and the Parliamentary Labour Party Education Group. In their 1962 pension campaign, the H.M.A. concentrated their efforts on a limited number of M.P.s known to be active on behalf of pensioners.

The House of Commons contains a large number of teachers, who can normally be relied upon, within the constraints of Party discipline, to express the associations' case in debate. All the associations anticipated no difficulty in having a Question put in the House, if they thought this necessary. The N.A.S., for example, used two Peers to press its amendments to the Remuneration of Teachers Act in 1965. In the 1950s, the Association had a list of M.P.s favourable to its request for representation on Burnham, and informed members of their electoral fortunes. By December 1969, the A.T.T.I. had eleven members in the House, with whom it held irregular meetings, and to whom it sent literature and policy statements. There were at least twenty N.U.T. members elected in 1959, and twenty-eight in 1964. The House in 1966 contained one hundred and thirteen teachers (eighty-four on the Labour side), of whom twenty-seven were N.U.T. members. The Union, seeking closer liaison, then arranged a regular meeting at least once a term, and now sends them appropriate briefing material on a regular basis.

Alone of the associations, the N.U.T. has formally sponsored candidates from the major Parties. It first did this in 1886, and first succeeded with the election of two of its leaders, one as a Liberal and one as a Unionist, in 1895. In 1964 the Union supported four Labour and two Conservative candidates; in 1966, three Labour and two Conservative. All but one Conservative were elected on both occasions. The N.A.S. too has given financial assistance to members standing in elections, and has developed close contacts with those elected. At present, two M.P.s are N.A.S. members; and the Association pays a Liberal M.P. a retainer as its Parliamentary advisor. Both the A.M.A. and N.A.H.T. have formally rejected the N.U.T. model. The 1965 A.M.A. Council referred back without debate a suggestion that the Association consider giving financial assistance to members standing in Elections; and in 1967 the Head Teachers rejected a similar call to explore the possibility of sponsoring at least two Parliamentary candidates.

On occasions, the larger associations have organised mass lobbies at the House, as part of nationally co-ordinated political campaigns. In 1931, the London association of the N.A.S. paraded down Whitehall to lobby M.P.s; and in 1961 a national lobby of N.A.S. members pressed the Government to admit the Association to the Burnham Committee. In 1969, the A.T.T.I. sent five hundred members to lobby their M.P.s in a campaign for higher salaries. The N.U.T. first organised such a Parliamentary lobby in 1875, when 'no fewer than 435 members of the House of Commons (were) interviewed by the officers of the Executive . . . or by representatives of local associations';[12] and in 1969 and 1970 M.P.s were lobbied at the House in support of an interim salary award.

THE WINNING OF PUBLIC SUPPORT

This is the most indirect of the three forms of behaviour traditionally taken by the associations in their search for influence. Each maintains regular links with the mass media, which are periodically mobilised in support of campaigns whose prime focus is always the Department, or Parliament, but never the 'educational public' alone.[13] They attempt to influence public opinion during campaigns on particular issues, on the assumption that favourable publicity is an asset when attemping to change the policy of politicians; and they maintain regular contacts with national and local press and radio, in order to generate a more long-term climate of opinion favourable to educational expansion. This second use of publicity campaigns was much expanded in the 1960s, and will be considered in Chapter 7. Publicity is more normally used for short-term goals.

As early as the N.U.T.'s first conference in 1870, a speaker proposed 'the publication of pamphlets to keep the public and Members of Parliament (informed of) the opinion of teachers';[14] and a student

[12] D. Thompson, op. cit. p. 87.
[13] The definition of 'public' varies with the campaign. Mass distribution of leaflets, as in the N.U.T. salary campaign of 1967, sets no limit on the width of the 'public' whose support is sought. But it is more normal for publicity material to be aimed, in the first instance, at what might be termed the 'educational public': that is, the daily (and educational) press, radio, television, M.P.s, councillors, educationalists and the other interest groups surrounding the D.E.S. (local authority associations, parent organisations, church bodies and organised capital and labour). Individual local authorities are often a target. Publicity in salary campaigns, for example, is often accompanied by local deputations to individual L.E.A.s, urging them to press the teachers' case on their national association.
[14] A. Tropp, op. cit. p. 112.

of the Union found such publicity one of the three 'successful methods of the National Union of Teachers' in its early years.[15] A century later, all the associations remain committed to the usefulness of public relations exercises. 'We are paid by public bodies', one teacher leader wrote in 1960, and they must 'necessarily be influenced by the attitude of their constituents.' A.M.A. Councils in 1955, 1963, and 1965 called for wider publicity for Association policy; and the A.T.T.I. drew up a memorandum in 1960 on the need for more publicity. Even the Headmasters' Association, which apparently held its first press conference only in 1958, was planning, by 1967, to extend publication of its *Review* to the general educational public.

The national organisation of the majority of the associations reflects this commitment to public relations. The N.A.H.T. appoints a special press officer for the period of its annual conference. The A.M.A. executive have an Organisation and Publicity Sub-committee, with an Honorary Press Secretary, and Press Correspondents at branch level. The N.A.S. has a Publications Committee of five members; the A.T.T.I. handle their publicity through an Information Officer, with the rank of Assistant Secretary; and the N.U.T. reorganised its Press Bureau in 1959, upgrading it to Departmental status with technical staff, as the new Publicity and Public Relations Committee of the Executive.

Each of the associations use their annual conference or council as a focus for press activity. Each holds press conferences on specific issues, and each writes letters to the press. The smaller associations release occasional policy statements through the press agencies; and amongst the larger associations publicity and public relations are conducted most systematically by the N.U.T. In a normal year, its publicity and public relations department maintains constant liaison with the press, radio and television. For example, in 1960, in addition to running publicity campaigns on teachers' salaries and on pensions for their dependants, the N.U.T.'s department organised publicity for the annual conference, the national sectional meetings and the Young Teachers' Conference; launched a film on the primary school, issued press statements on a wide range of topics from Government reports to booklets on the teaching of science; and

---

[15] D. Thompson, op. cit. p. 87. The others were (1) pressure brought to bear on the Department of Education and M.P.s, and (2) direct representation in Parliament.

gave advice to the B.B.C. on a drama documentary on secondary education.

In particular, each salary campaign has come to involve a publicity drive. That of the N.A.S. in 1964 involved mass meetings in seven regional centres and in London. Similarly in 1969, the teachers' demand for an interim pay award was supported by a full-page advertisement by the N.U.T. in the *Guardian* and *The Times*. The Union's 1967 publicity campaign may be taken as typical. It published two leaflets early in the year, printing 30,000 copies of one and 150,000 of the other. It later printed half a million copies of a third leaflet and 50,000 of a fourth. Local associations issued these to the local press, local organisations, and the general public. When the Union undertook militant action in the autumn, national press conferences were held on the plans for sanctions, on the results of local referenda, and at all the later stages of the campaign. Local press conferences and mass meetings were held in sanction areas, Union officials appeared on national television and radio, and local officials took part in local radio and television coverage.

3

The Limits of Traditional Pressure

These traditional forms of behaviour share three characteristics. They are used, with only slight differences of emphasis, by all the teachers' associations, and not just by the already well-documented N.U.T. All have established close working relationships with the Department; all have proved willing to resort to Parliamentary pressure; and each maintains contacts with the mass media. But the larger associations attach greater importance, and resort more frequently, to Parliamentary pressure than do the smaller; and the N.U.T. has a more sophisticated machinery for public relations than have any of the other associations.

Moreover, the full range of traditional behaviour was established early and remained unchanged through the 1950s. In the 1870s, the N.U.T. sent deputations to the Department, lobbied M.P.s and contacted the press; and in the 1950s, all the associations used all of these forms of behaviour in their continuing search for influence.

Lastly, there have been changes of emphasis within these traditional forms of behaviour over time. The associations go less to Parliament, and more to the Department, than they did in the nineteenth century; and with the Department, contacts are more frequent and less formal than in the early years of each association. This is particularly true of the associations initially denied easy access – the N.U.T. and N.A.S. – but it applies in differing degrees to them all.

The strengths and weaknesses of these traditional strategies and tactics were most clearly demonstrated by two major campaigns in which they were used by the teachers' associations in the 1960s: in the joint campaign for a shared-cost dependants' pension scheme, and in the N.U.T.'s Parliamentary campaign against Sir Edward Boyle's imposition of salary scales in 1963. By looking in detail at these – which are in fact only two of a large number of occasions on which the teachers' associations relied entirely on their traditional strategies and tactics – the motives which prompted the associations to seek supplementary forms of behaviour should begin to become clear.

The campaign for a dependants' pension scheme is particularly illuminating for a number of reasons. It was almost entirely an exercise between the teachers' associations, the Ministry of Education, and the national associations of local authorities; and as such, focused on the very centre of the relationship between organised teachers and Government. For the associations' direct and regular contact with the Department is their prime means of influence. All other strategies and tactics that they adopt are related to this, as attempts to strengthen their hand in direct dealings with the Department. Even the most virulent Parliamentary campaign has as its aim a change of policy by the Department that will require fresh direct consultation with the teachers' associations. It is to the nature of these consultative processes that a study of the campaign for a dependants' pension scheme draws attention.

Moreover, as a campaign, it was typical of the form which relations with the Department habitually take; repeated meetings over a long period, the use of deputations and working parties, and the search for acceptable compromise. The object of the campaign was a matter of crucial importance to the associations and high on the agendas of successive teachers' conferences. So any lack of influence by the teachers' associations here cannot be explained away in terms of any lack of commitment by them to the need for a shared-cost dependants' pension scheme. Equally, the associations were united in their demand for such a scheme – a unity rare in teachers' politics. So any lack of influence cannot be explained away in terms of divisions between them. Finally, and as a result, the campaign brings out clearly the limits on the effectiveness of the traditional forms of teacher behaviour, limits which in the 1960s inspired a search for new or revived strategies and tactics. For these reasons, and for the light it throws on the decision-making processes of the Department of Education, it is worth considering in detail here.

THE CAMPAIGN FOR A SHARED-COST DEPENDANTS' PENSION SCHEME

By 1960, the teachers' associations had been campaigning for a shared-cost dependants' pension scheme for eleven years.[1] In their

[1] A shared-cost scheme was one whose costs were shared *equally* by the teachers and their employers.

initial approach in 1949, they had found the Government (who had just negotiated such a scheme with their civil servants) favourable to the idea. But in 1951 the local authorities had made clear their unwillingness to participate in any shared-cost scheme, and the new Government had refused to finance one unless the local authorities also contributed. Neither the local authorities nor the Government altered their positions in the 1950s, in spite of repeated meetings with the teachers' associations. In 1956 the teachers were offered a scheme financed by themselves alone; but this was rejected by a special conference of the N.U.T., and so not implemented by the Minister, Sir David Eccles.

The campaign reopened in 1960 when, on the initiative of the A.M.A., Sir David Eccles met a deputation from the N.U.T., A.T.T.I. and Joint Four. The Minister was sympathetic but firm. He argued that improved pension benefits could be given only at the expense of salary increases, unless the local authorities reconsidered their position and contributed to the costs involved. The policy of the local authorities had to change if the teachers were to achieve their objective. Since the Minister was unwilling to encourage them to make that change, it was left to the teachers to try.

Even before this meeting, the N.U.T. executive had announced a campaign to secure a shared-cost pension scheme. In this, they had the support of both the A.T.T.I. and the Joint Four; so that action at local level involved members of all these associations, and at times, of the N.A.S. also. The campaign was specifically aimed at the local authorities, in an attempt to persuade them to share the cost of such a scheme. Each local association of the Union petitioned its L.E.A. through the drawing up of a petition signed by members and non-members alike, and by deputations from all the local associations of teachers. Deputations and petitions waited on individual local authorities from the early summer and through the autumn of 1960; and by December, approximately 200,000 teachers had signed petitions, and thirty-three local authorities had expressed some measure of definite support for the Union's proposals.[2]

The initial reaction of the national associations of local autho-

[2] I.e. approximately two-thirds of the teaching profession signed the petition, and one-fifth of the local authorities gave some measure of support.

rities was to stand firm. When they met the teachers' associations in February 1961, the authorities refused to discuss a shared-cost scheme for the teachers alone. All that they would agree was that they would discuss the teachers' request within the context of local government generally. Following these discussions, they would meet the teachers' associations again. They did not do so until December 1962.

From the winter of 1961 to the late summer of 1962 the teachers maintained their pressure only informally and through the publicity of their conferences; and by 1962, dissatisfaction at these conferences was general. Twice in 1961, the teachers' associations reminded the authorities of their undertaking to reconvene the February meeting, only to be told that they were not yet ready for further discussions. Yet there had been consultations amongst the local authorities after the February meeting, but these had merely 'confirmed the view previously held... that the contributions to a pension scheme for widows, orphans and dependants should be wholly borne by teachers as was already the case in local government generally'.[3] The campaign of 1960 to change the policy of the local authorities had failed.

To break the deadlock, the teachers' associations turned once more to the Minister. Such an approach would have been pointless without new proposals from one side or the other. That this meeting was more productive than any other reflected no easing of Government policy. On the contrary, the new Minister adopted a position more hostile to the teachers' demand than any Minister before him. The meeting was productive only because the teachers' associations, in the light of a report on the pensions of dependants of teachers in Scotland, abandoned their immediate objective – one of a shared-cost scheme – as this had been understood in the 1950s.

As in England, the Scottish local authorities refused to participate in a shared-cost scheme, but they were willing, with the Scottish Education Department, to pay the administrative costs of a scheme otherwise financed by the teachers. In the scheme proposed by the Scottish working party, the teachers were to pay 2% of their gross salary, on which they would receive income tax relief to reduce their average contribution to 1.4%.

Within a week of the report's publication, the N.U.T.'s General Secretary asked the new Minister, Sir Edward Boyle, to meet a

[3] *C.C.A. Gazette Supplement,* January 1963, p. 7.

deputation of the eight major teachers' associations. At this meeting, in October 1962, the Minister was unwilling to commit the Government to the Scottish report. He recognised that the L.E.A.s might be prepared to administer a scheme financed totally by the teachers, but he would not urge them to do so. Indeed, he insisted that any scheme which involved sharing the cost would have to be ruled out; and this veto on a shared-cost scheme would hold good even if the authorities offered more than just the administrative costs. For the Government now took the view that if it met the teachers' demands, repercussions on the pensions of other public sector employees would be too great.

Sir Edward Boyle suggested that the teachers go back to the local authority associations; and at a meeting in December 1962, the local authorities accepted the Scottish proposals as a basis for negotiation. Though they insisted that no additional funds would be available for a widows' and orphans' pension scheme, they were prepared to consider paying the administrative costs of a scheme otherwise totally financed by the teachers. On this basis, an unofficial working party was created, to explore the possibilities of an acceptable scheme. This working party first met in March 1963, and twice thereafter.

The association conferences of 1963 saw the readjustment of the teachers' position in the face of local authority and Ministerial intransigence. In January, the A.M.A. resolution urging the executive 'to press for pensions for the widows and dependants of teachers' contained no reference to a shared-cost scheme; and the significance of this was clear in the debate. The A.M.A. was conceding defeat, for the moment, on its ultimate aim. So apparently was the N.U.T. at its Easter conference. Union members had voted a motion demanding a civil service type scheme to the head of the conference agenda. At conference, the executive attempted for the first time to delete all reference to a shared-cost scheme, in favour of one only 'acceptable to the profession'. Opposition speakers from the floor stressed what the executive had not tried to hide, namely that they 'had in mind a scheme which would be financed entirely by teachers... It meant a complete abandonment of the principle of shared contribution.'[4] Even so, the executive amendment was carried 'on a show of hands'. The A.T.T.I. conference also left their objective as a scheme 'acceptable to the

[4] *The Teacher*, 26 April 1963, p. 27.

profession'; but a similar attempt by the N.A.H.T. executive at their Whitsun conference produced a rare defeat from the floor.

The report of the unofficial working party was ready by July 1963. Its major recommendation was that the Minister should establish an official working party, to prepare a detailed scheme financed by the teachers but administered at the expense of the Ministry and local authorities. The Government accepted this recommendation, and appointed a working party with the terms of reference suggested.[5] This second working party reported in February 1965.

In two ways, its proposals fell short of the teachers' goals: on the question of the sharing of costs, and in its treatment of the older teacher. Throughout, the teachers' associations pressed for a shared-cost scheme. The N.U.T. executive were told: 'we asked for that time and again, and on every occasion we got an unfavourable answer. On the last occasion we mentioned it, each of the representatives of the authorities individually expressed opposition to such a scheme.'[6] The Government and the local authorities were persuaded however to concede tax relief on the teachers' contribution, and to pay the administrative costs.

The teachers' associations, led by the N.A.S., also pressed for financial help for the older teacher, who faced heavy costs if he was to 'buy his way' into the scheme. But the authorities' representatives were unwilling to commit their organisations, and agreed only to approach the Secretary of State who, at the last meeting of the working party in January 1965, rejected the teachers' demand. A later approach to his successor brought a similar reply.

As in 1956, the Secretary of State would proceed only with majority teacher support; and of the associations, only the N.A.S. rejected the scheme (because of its treatment of the older teacher). The executive of the A.M.A., though regretting the rejection of a shared-cost scheme, recommended acceptance; and the A.T.T.I.

---

[5] The participation of the N.U.T. in this official working party, and perhaps therefore the existence of the working party itself, was jeopardised by a rank and file revolt at the N.U.T. conference in 1964. There, in spite of very strong opposition from the Union's executive, the conference reversed the policy of the previous year, and insisted on the establishment of a shared-cost scheme. The N.U.T. only joined the working party after reference to a shared-cost scheme was deleted from Union policy at a special conference later in the year.

[6] *The Teacher*, 12 February 1965, p. 4 (Mr Barton).

voted in favour of the proposals at its conference in June. But as in 1956, the final power of veto lay with the N.U.T. as the largest association; and its reaction was long in doubt. Its executive took three meetings before recommending acceptance; and at the Easter conference, a motion referring the decision to a special conference was defeated by the minute margin of 133 votes out of 192,000.

In 1965, the Secretary of State announced that, given the 'very broad consensus' existing in favour of the scheme, he would introduce legislation; and the resulting Teachers Superannuation Act came into operation on 1 April 1966. 45,000 serving male teachers (approximately one male teacher in four) chose to buy their way in, and by 1967 a motion seeking an improved widows' pension scheme failed to be voted onto that year's N.U.T. conference agenda. The issued was settled.

THE N.U.T.'S PARLIAMENTARY CAMPAIGN OF 1963

It is also worth looking briefly at one attempt by the N.U.T. to shape Departmental policy by Parliamentary action: its attempt to prevent Ministerial imposition of salary scales in 1963. The attempt followed the failure of direct approaches to the Ministry, and it also failed.

This political campaign must be seen in its context. Since 1920, the teachers' associations and the national associations of local authorities had negotiated teachers' salaries in the Burnham Committees, on which the Department of Education was not represented. Between the wars, the President of the Board of Education had occasionally intervened in the workings of the Committees, but after 1944 the Minister had no formal role there. His representatives attended only to supply information; and his powers were limited by the 1944 Act to the outright approval or rejection of the Committee's recommendations. Ministers in 1954 and in 1959 had made known their dislike of features of Burnham settlements, but neither had been prepared to force the Committee to revise its proposals.

In 1961, this autonomy of the Burnham Committees from Ministerial intervention was challenged by the Minister, Sir David Eccles, in the opening stages of Selwyn Lloyd's 'pay pause'. In his speech announcing the pause, the Chancellor of the Exchequer mentioned the teachers specifically, informing the House of the Government's opposition to both the size and the distribution of the Burnham settlement then under discussion. Accordingly, Sir David Eccles instructed the Committee to reduce its proposed basic scale; and the conflict between the Minister and the Committee went on into the autumn of 1961.[7]

Both Selwyn Lloyd and Sir David Eccles made clear that, though the timing of their intervention reflected the immediate balance of payments crisis, it was also a product of a longer-term Government desire to participate more closely in the workings of the Burnham Committee; and by October the Minister was planning a Bill to strengthen his powers of salary determination. This was delayed only when the Burnham Committee agreed to implement the Minister's cuts; and lengthy talks on the possible restructuring of the Committee were then held between Departmental officials and the national associations of local authorities and teachers. But in March 1962, the Minister announced that he was postponing any change in the Burnham machinery until the Government's own machinery for incomes policy had taken a more definite shape. This decision was taken by the N.U.T. as a major victory, a victory that was however called into serious question when Sir David Eccles' successor at the Ministry rejected the next Burnham settlement. In Sir Edward Boyle's action the teachers' associations understandably saw a revival of the earlier policy of Government intervention; and this, as much as the specific salary changes which the Minister proposed, explains the vigour of the N.U.T.'s campaign against him.[8]

Sir Edward Boyle announced his rejection of the Burnham settlement in February 1963. His action divided the teachers' associations. The Headmasters' Association gave him their public support; the A.M.A. and N.A.S. condemned both the substance and nature of his intervention, but welcomed the prospect of a review of the Burnham machinery; and the N.U.T., with the A.T.T.I., remained as the champion of the old Burnham Committee, whose teachers' side it dominated.

The N.U.T. organised a Parliamentary campaign, to coincide

[7] On this, see Chapter 6, pp. 64–67.
[8] See R. D. Coates, 'The teachers' associations and the restructuring of Burnham', *British Journal of Educational Studies* (June 1972, pp. 192–204).

with the various stages of Sir Edward Boyle's Remuneration of Teachers Bill, through which the Minister was to impose his own salary scale for a two-year period. In defence of the rejected agreement and the autonomy of the Burnham Committee, the Union briefed its sponsored M.P.s, who put a number of Parliamentary Questions. Its General Secretary met leading Labour spokesmen on the day before a major Commons debate on education, and later addressed a meeting of 100 Conservative backbenchers. The President of the Union announced that he would stand against the Minister in the next General Election; and in this, he had the support of the Union's executive.[9] Local associations were twice asked to make direct approaches to their local M.P.; a press campaign was launched; and local and regional protest meetings were organised to coincide with the Second Reading of the Minister's Bill.

On 27 March, 6,000 Union members, well briefed at headquarters, lobbied 376 M.P.s at the House. Each M.P. was sent a short memorandum by the Union in time for the Bill's Second Reading. A smaller 'lobby in depth' was held on the day of the second reading, when 1,000 selected Union members saw individual M.P.s at Westminster. The lobbies concentrated on the Party in power, and between them covered 257 of the 321 Conservatives, including all but 19 of the 97 in marginal constituencies. The Union found 'considerable misgivings among a substantial minority of Conservative M.P.s about Sir Edward Boyle's action, and substantial support for the view that in any new negotiating machinery, teachers' negotiating rights should be safeguarded and arbitration provided'.[10] More than 60 M.P.s signed a Commons motion in the name of a Union-sponsored M.P., condemning the Minister's action. The Parliamentary Labour Party voted solidly against the Bill at its Second Reading, and all the amendments which the Union required were moved at the Committee Stage by Opposition M.P.s.

The Minister withstood this pressure. The only change that he

---

[9] The scheme was abandoned only when the Union's conference in 1963 failed to provide more than the narrowest majority in its favour.

[10] *N.U.T. Annual Report 1963*, p. 92. Only one Conservative voted against the Government at the Second Reading; though 'at least another eight abstained or deliberately stayed away'. S. E. Finer, *Anonymous Empire* (London, Pall Mall Press, 2nd ed., 1966), p. 97.

made in his Order was to give an extra £10 to teachers in special schools, and to those in charge of special classes in normal schools! Otherwise, the salary scales operating between April 1963 and March 1965 were those which Sir Edward Boyle, and not the Burnham Committee, had decided; and which had been announced before the N.U.T.'s Parliamentary campaign was fully under way.

There is a postscript to this Parliamentary confrontation. In talks in the summer of 1963, and in 1964, the N.U.T. continued to oppose any Ministerial participation in the workings of the Burnham Committee. Yet, ironically, it was left to a Union-sponsored M.P., as the Labour Government's first Secretary of State for Education and Science, to introduce the Remuneration of Teachers Act 1965, by which the D.E.S. entered the Burnham Committee on the Management side.[11]

THE EFFECTIVENESS OF TRADITIONAL FORMS OF TEACHER PRESSURE

The persistent feature of both campaigns is that of failure to achieve initial goals. This is clearest in the confrontation with Sir Edward Boyle; but it is equally true of the campaign for a dependants' pension scheme. The associations set out to win a shared-cost scheme. They could have had a scheme totally financed by teachers as early as 1956. The 1965 settlement improved on this, but it was not the shared-cost scheme for which they had asked.

The failure here was not total. Without a teachers' campaign, it is unlikely that any dependants' pension scheme would have been introduced; and the level of contribution (after tax) required from the teachers was only slightly higher in the 1965 Act than in the shared-cost scheme of the civil servants. But the willingness of the Government to provide a pension scheme was clear by 1956. The campaign of 1960 was not to win a pension scheme, but to win

[11] The Union-sponsorship of Michael Stewart did not prevent him adopting a Bill only marginally different from that which the N.U.T. had opposed in talks with his Conservative predecessor. Yet his sponsorship affected the N.U.T. – they initially greeted the Bill as a considerable improvement on the Conservative proposals. By October 1967, the N.U.T. executive had reverted to its old position – of demanding the removal of the Secretary of State from the Management Panel of Burnham.

one whose costs were shared equally between teachers and their employers; and in this, it failed.

The mass petitioning of the L.E.A.s in 1960 failed. Talks opened only after the Scottish report, and only after a major concession of policy by the teachers. The shift of position by the teachers' executives at their conferences in 1963 indicated the extent of this concession, as did the N.U.T. executive's reaction to their defeat at conference in 1964. The teachers conceded defeat on their prime objective of a shared-cost scheme before the working parties began.

This defeat was written into the terms of reference of the unofficial working party. These embodied the local authorities' position, which they were determined to defend;[12] and once negotiations were opened, the teachers could not easily escape these limitations. The N.U.T. executive rightly took their defeat at conference in 1964 as an attempt to break out of the constraints imposed on the official working party at its creation, and Sir Ronald Gould saw the likely outcome of this.

> It might easily be that the local authorities would say 'it is useless to proceed any further because neither our people nor the Government are prepared to accept a scheme similar to that of the civil service'. Then obviously the only course of action would be pressure on Parliament, pressure on the Minister of Education, to try to secure the reopening of negotiations on a new basis.[13]

The working party's terms of reference reflected the distribution of power within the education sector. They were not the cause of the teachers' failure, but its manifestation. They were the insurmountable obstacle precisely because the teachers lacked the power to moderate the policy of either the authorities or the Government that they embodied.

In this campaign, and in the Parliamentary confrontation of 1963, Ministerial resolve was strengthened by Government policy commitments outside the education sector. Sir Edward Boyle's unwill-

---

[12] The A.M.C. were told, 'your representatives on the working party... concerned themselves mainly with ensuring that the wishes of the Association had been observed and did not take a major part in framing the scheme'. (*The Municipal Review Supplement*, 1965, p. 169.)

[13] The General Secretary of the N.U.T., in *The Teacher*, 10 April 1964, p. 4.

ingness to abandon his Remuneration of Teachers Bill was at least partly educational in motive, but it was strengthened by its part in the wider Government policy of gaining control of the rate of growth of money wages. This, as Sir David Eccles admitted, was the long-term aim behind the initial intervention in Burnham in 1961; and whatever Sir Edward Boyle's motives, was one product of the Ministerial involvement in Burnham that is confrontation with the Committee precipitated.

These external constraints on bargaining within the education sector were clearest in the campaign for a dependants' pension scheme. The teachers' demand for a shared-cost scheme was rejected because of its implications for Government policy outside the education sector. The authorities' argument always, and Sir Edward Boyle's in 1962, was that the repercussions on other public employees of a decision to give the teachers a shared-cost scheme would be too great. It was these fears of repercussions in other parts of the public sector which left Government and local authorities unresponsive to the teachers' pressure; and the associations were thus frustrated by the implication of their demands for power relationships (in this case, between other public sector employees and the Government) in which they did not participate, and which their traditional strategy and tactics did not permit them to influence.

These two examples of the activity of the associations begin to make clear the limits on the effectiveness of the traditional forms of their pressure. To guarantee influence to the teachers' associations even in the long term,[14] these forms of behaviour required two things of the Department of Education. First, they required that the Department should not be so committed to preconceived policy that it would withstand sustained pressure by the associations. For the Parliamentary campaign of 1963 indicated the impotence of Parliament before a committed Department; yet, under the traditional forms of their pressure, it was only to Parliament that the teachers' associations could turn in their attempt to shake that Deparmental commitment. In 1963, neither the N.U.T.'s pressure

---

[14] As the campaign for a dependants' pension scheme indicated, success should be measured over a period. It was a feature of the traditional forms of teacher pressure that initial failure was countered by a repetition of pressure on the same issue, in the hope of a change of Government policy over time.

on the Conservative backbenchers, nor the support of the Opposition, could break Sir Edward Boyle's resolve.

Second, and more crucial, the traditional forms of teacher pressure required that the goals of the teachers' associations should not have implications for Government policy outside the education sector, since such implications could restrict the freedom of the Department to respond to the associations' demands. The traditional concentration of organised teachers on decision-making processes within the system of educational administration alone, rested on the assumption that the D.E.S. was in some sense free to take the decisions that the associations required, unconstrained by Government policy in other sectors. Yet the campaign for a dependants' pension scheme indicated the absence, on this issue at least, of this D.E.S. autonomy. The Department did not grant a shared-cost pension scheme because of the implications of such a scheme for Government policy on pensions in other areas of the public sector.

These findings can be stated more generally. When the Department of Education and Science is already committed to a particular educational policy it is less open to the impact of reasoned argument by the teachers' associations, and less susceptible to the threat of public debate through Parliamentary pressure. When it is constrained by wider Government policy, its freedom to manoeuvre in the face of the teachers' demands is limited by relationships of power between Government and organised groups outside the education system. Indeed, often the Department is committed to a particular policy precisely because its freedom to manoeuvre is limited by wider relationships of power. So, in the campaign for a dependants' pension scheme, Government hostility to a shared-cost scheme grew as the Department of Education became convinced that concessions to the teachers would have repercussions for the pension schemes of other public sector employees.

These traditional forms of teacher pressure were still much used in the 1960s. But the willingness of the associations in the last decade to *supplement* them stemmed from the increasing absence of this second requirement – of D.E.S. autonomy. For as will be argued in the next chapter, Government policy in the 1960s reduced the range of issues on which the D.E.S. was free to respond to the reasoned arguments of the teachers' associations. The associations then turned to new or revived strategies and tactics, in order to strengthen their position before the Department, and to win influence over policy made outside the education sector. These limits on the effectiveness of the traditional forms of the associations' behaviour, and the pattern of new strategies and tactics adopted, will be clearest when considered in terms of the relationships of power within which the teachers' associations seek influence.

4

Relationships of Power and the Changing Context of Bargaining

The Department of Education has never enjoyed total freedom of decision-making within national government. As a spending Department, it has always competed with other spending Departments for available Government resources;[1] and its position here is directly analogous to that of the Ministry of Health that Eckstein described, in that 'over all [its] activities involving the expenditure of money, and bearing upon economic policy in the larger sense looms the omnipresent Treasury, the chief co-ordinating department, with its comprehensive powers over departmental budgets, and its formal power to give or deny prior approval to a departmental project having a financial aspect'.[2]

For money spent on education means real resources diverted from alternative uses; from use by other public services; and from use within the private sector. To win these resources for education, the D.E.S. has to compete with the spokesmen of other public services and those of the private sector. That is, it is engaged in a relationship of power with each. And to use these resources, once gained, the Department faces a third relationship of power: that between itself and the interest groups that surround it – the local authorities and their associations, the teachers' associations, the churches, parent and voluntary bodies.

This means that the teachers' associations themselves face three relationships of power, each more general than the one before. The

[1] Technically, the L.E.A.s rather than the D.E.S. spend public money on education, and very little expenditure passes directly through the Department. But the D.E.S. is intimately involved in the negotiation of the Rate Support Grant; and the ability of the local authorities to provide educational facilities to the standards set by the Department depends on the size of that Grant. So education as a public service – with the D.E.S. as its national spokesman – is in competition with other public services for the resources available.

[2] H. Eckstein, *Pressure Group Politics* (London, Allen and Unwin, 1960), p. 54.

most immediate is that between the D.E.S. and its interest groups; then, that between the education system and other public services; and finally, that between the public and the private sectors. Indeed, these power-relationships can be usefully seen as concentric circles expanding from the former to the latter; in that the more general relationship of power is an external limit on the more specific one, and is itself constrained by relationships that are more general still. For the power-balance between the Government and the private sector determines the size, and to a degree the distribution, of the resources available to the public sector; and decisions taken within the public sector on the distribution of these resources between public services fixes the amount available for use within the education sector itself.

To each relationship of power corresponds a level of policy, and points of decision-making within the structure of Government. From the relationship between the D.E.S. and its interest groups comes *education policy*, determined in negotiations centred on the Department. From the relationship of the education sector to other areas of public activity comes *policy on the distribution of Government expenditure*, determined in Ministerial negotiations within the Cabinet.[3] And from the relationship between the public and private sectors comes *national economic policy*, determined in consultations between major Government Departments[4] and organised labour and capital (both industrial and financial, national and international). Each lower level of policy operates within a supply of resources determined at a higher level. So the size of the public

---

[3] Decision-making here in the 1950s was piecemeal (see Plowden, *Control of Public Expenditure*, Cmnd. 1432, 1961, p. 5), but since 1965 'for planning and decision purposes, public expenditure...is divided into functional blocks. The defence budget, roads, housing, education, health and welfare, benefits and assistance account for about three-quarters of the total. Since 1965, the intended method of working has been for the Government to decide the total of public expenditure which can be afforded in future years, and then to divide this up between the main functions, leaving the Minister in charge of each function to consider how the resources within his block can best be used.' (J. Bray, *Decision in Government* (London, Gollancz, 1970), p. 125.)

[4] Primarily, in the 1960s, the Treasury, the Department of Economic Affairs, the Department of Employment and Productivity (the old Ministry of Labour), and the Board of Trade, within the general oversight of the Cabinet and Prime Minister.

sector is one concern of national economic policy, and the resources available for educational advance are the product of Government policy on the distribution of the amount of public expenditure so determined.

With these relationships isolated, and with the levels of policy that they generate understood, it is now possible to redefine the limits on the traditional forms of teacher pressure. The teachers' traditional strategy – of a preoccupation with decision-making centres within the education sector alone – involved no direct attempt by their associations to influence *either* policy on the distribution of Government expenditure, *or* national economic policy. On the contrary, the associations traditionally left the task of obtaining sufficient resources for educational advance to the political head of the Education Department.

So that even where the Government's education policy was not at variance with the associations' goals, this strategy could still only be effective to the degree that the Secretary of State for Education and Science was able to win sufficient resources in negotiations with his Cabinet colleagues. In addition, to offer even the possibility of influence, this traditional strategy required that the issues on which the teachers' associations pressed the Department were neither decided as part of, nor had implications for, national economic policy. It was the increasing absence of these two requirements that prompted the adoption of new or revived forms of behaviour by organised teachers in the 1960s.

For the teachers' associations adopted new strategies and tactics in response to changes that they saw in the relationships of power within which they sought influence. As a result of a changing pattern of Government policy, they came to recognise (in varying degrees), both the need for influence on the distribution of public expenditure and on the formulation of national economic policy, and the need for new tactics within the education sector itself.

THE CHANGING PATTERN OF GOVERNMENT POLICY

Decision-making on the distribution of public expenditure and on national economic policy became more relevant for policy-making within the education sector, and more visible and accessible to the teachers' associations seeking influence there, as a result of four sets of Government policy in the 1960s. The distribution of public expenditure became more relevant as a by-product of the Government's commitment to educational expansion after 1955. National economic policy impinged directly on the D.E.S. through the development and application of incomes policy after 1961. The significance of both became more visible to the teachers' associations because of Government attempts at national planning and incomes control; and became more accessible to them through the willingness of Governments to involve a peak organisation of labour in both the formal machinery of national planning and in regular consultations on the course of national economic policy, including policy on incomes control. And at the end of the decade, these external constraints on decision-making by the D.E.S. were underlined by education cuts, and by restrictions on the growth rate of educational expenditure that were occasioned by balance of payments crises. Each of these policy developments changed the context within which the teachers' associations determined their strategies and tactics.

Educational expansion

Conservative Governments after 1955 allowed educational expenditure to grow faster than national income. The period 1955–64, unlike any that preceded it, was characterised by sustained expansion in teacher training, in further and higher education, and in secondary education. Educational expenditure that was only 2.5% of the Gross National Product between the wars, and only 3.2% in the mid 1950s, had reached 5% a decade later, and nearly 6% by 1969.[5]

This expansion, as Table 2 shows, was financed partly by expanding the percentage of G.N.P. entering the public sector, and partly by redistributing expenditure within the public sector itself: running down defence as a percentage of G.N.P., and holding constant other areas of social policy, namely public housing and the national health service. Proportionately less of G.N.P. was spent on public housing in 1963 than in 1955; and less than an additional half per cent of the national product went to the national health service. Yet education expanded by 1.5% of G.N.P. in this period.

[5] J. Vaizey and J. Sheehan, *Resources for Education* (London, Allen and Unwin, 1968), p. 2.

Table 2. *Government expenditure as a percentage of G.N.P. 1955–68*

Date	Total public expenditure	Education	Health	Housing	Defence
1955	36.9	3.2	3.5	2.5	9.4
1960	41.5	4.0	3.8	2.2	7.2
1963	43.0	4.7	3.8	2.2	7.0
1966	46.5	5.4	4.2	2.9	6.7
1968	52.1	5.9	4.6	3.0	6.7

Educational expansion did not halt under the Labour Government before 1968, but the sector no longer monopolised expansion in the social services. Housing, at 3% of G.N.P. by 1968, was consistently half a percentage higher in the second half of the 1960s than in the first. Expenditure on the health service showed a parallel increase. As is clear from Table 3, the distribution of Government social spending moved strongly in favour of education between 1955 and 1963, but since then this distribution has stabilised, and there has been expansion on all three policy fronts. As Vaizey has noted, 'the pressure on resources has increased' and 'the growth of education is now running into severe limitations after a period of unprecedented growth',[6] both because of this competition from other expanding public services, and because (as will be shown later) of limitations on the growth rate of public expenditure in total.

But if the supply of resources for education is likely to grow less rapidly in the 1970s, the demand for education is not. The school

Table 3. *The distribution of Government expenditure on education, health and public housing 1955–68*

Date	Education	Health	Public housing
1955	36.5	36.9	26.6
1960	40.4	38.0	21.6
1963	44.1	35.6	20.3
1966	42.8	33.8	23.4
1968	43.7	33.9	22.4

[6] Vaizey and Sheehan, op. cit. pp. 1 and vii.

population of England and Wales, which increased only from 6 m. to 7.2 m. in the half-century ending in 1955, grew to just under 8 m. by 1967, and is expected to approach 10 m. by 1980. In addition, a growing percentage of this rising tide of enrolments is concentrating in high-cost education areas – in sixth forms and in further and higher education. In 1955, less than 2% of children in school were over sixteen. By 1967 that percentage had risen to nearly 4%, and is likely to be in the region of 7% by 1980. Between 1955 and 1967, the number of full-time students receiving further education – including those training to be teachers – more than doubled.

Because of a persistently low rate of economic growth through the 1960s, the maintenance of prevailing educational standards in the face of this rising *quantity* of demand required that education should receive a growing percentage of G.N.P. (of probably at least 8% by 1980). If the *quality* of educational provision was to improve also, education required an even greater share of the national product.[7] In both cases, this could be achieved only by holding back the relative growth rate of Government expenditure on other public services, or by expanding still further the percentage of G.N.P. consumed by the public sector. In each case, with educational expenditure on this scale and facing this growth of demand, the provision of adequate resources required that education be a major priority of Governments. It was the realisation of this, and of the consequent growing need to gain a voice in the determination of the overall distribution of Government expenditure, that prompted the teachers' associations to create the 1963 Campaign For Education and the later Council for Educational Advance.

Incomes policies

Interest in incomes policy extends over much of the post-war period. Between 1948 and 1950, Sir Stafford Cripps attempted to limit the growth rate of money incomes to that of physical output; and the Conservative Government in 1956 called for a 'prices plateau' and for wage restraint. In 1957, it established a Council on Prices,

[7] The only method of maintaining the quality of educational provision without a greater share of G.N.P. would be a considerable increase in productivity within the sector itself, a matter of great controversy and difficulty.

Productivity and Incomes, to report on broad changes in these areas; and the final report of this Council in 1961 stressed the advantages of some form of incomes policy.

Yet in the development of incomes policy, as in the attempts at national planning, Selwyn Lloyd's Chancellorship marks a sharp change in Government policy. For only from 1961 did the Treasury become systematically involved in the determination of income movements, a process begun by Lloyd's announcement of a 'pay pause' that lasted until March 1962. This was followed by the policy of the 'guiding light' of first $2-2\frac{1}{4}\%$, and then $3-3\frac{1}{2}\%$, and by the creation of the National Incomes Commission. In 1965, the Labour Government created the National Board for Prices and Incomes, announced an incomes norm of $3\frac{1}{2}\%$, and specified the conditions under which it could be exceeded. From July 1966, a six-month statutory 'wage freeze' was followed by a 'period of severe restraint' with a nil norm, by a $3\frac{1}{2}\%$ norm from July 1967, and by one of $4\frac{1}{2}\%$ from January 1970. By then, only the non-statutory elements of the policy remained; and even these were abandoned by the incoming Conservative Government in 1970.

Teachers have always been subject to an incomes policy of sorts, in that the size of any increase – even in the 1950s – had to be accepted by the Minister of Education, and hence by the Treasury. But the incomes policies that the associations experienced after 1961 (and especially that of Selwyn Lloyd, and those of the Labour Government after the July measures of 1966) differed in kind, form and in application from the pattern of salary negotiations experienced by teachers in the 1950s.

They differed in kind in that, for the first time, teachers' salary negotiations were affected by their likely impact on private sector wage settlements, and not just on the wage settlements of other public, and especially local government, employees. They differed in form in that each emerged from a publicly visible decision-making process – from consultations between the Government, the T.U.C. and the peak organisations of business – from which the teachers' associations were clearly isolated (as indeed they had been from the private discussions between the Ministry of Education and the Treasury in the 1950s) but to which a channel of access, through the T.U.C., was now available.[8]

[8] Lloyd's 'pay pause' alone was not introduced after consultation with the peak organisations of business and labour, and later Governments

The incomes policies of the 1960s were applied to public employees, including teachers, more rigorously than to employees in the private sector. In 1961, Selwyn Lloyd deliberately applied the 'pay pause' to the public sector as an example to the private. Even Labour's policy, though more equitable in intention and more sophisticated in application, was in reality little different. Machinery created to plan a socially just structure of prices and incomes in an expanding economy became, in a period of economic retrenchment, a mechanism of wages control rigidly enforced in the Burnham Committee, whilst applied with dwindling rigour to the private sector. Indeed by 1969, incomes policy was applied unevenly within the public sector itself, with the norm being maintained in the Burnham Committee when ignored for other public employees such as dustmen and firemen.

The pattern of teacher militancy that characterised the decade was a direct response to the teachers' experience of these successive incomes policies; and the move by the larger associations into the T.U.C. reflected their desire to participate in the formation of national economic policy in general, and incomes policy in particular, that so affected negotiations within the Burnham Committee. This last move – the search for an alliance with organised labour, received a greater impetus through the development of national planning in the 1960s.

National planning

For a while in the mid-1960s, it appeared that rather more than the rate of increase of salaries would be determined in consultative processes outside the education sector, from which the teachers' associations would be excluded. For the Conservatives in 1962 began an attempt at indicative planning that the Labour Government continued; and under each, this took the form of widespread consultation with the peak organisations of business and labour to produce national and sectoral targets for growth.

The Conservatives began, in February 1962, by creating the National Economic Development Council, through which senior ministers and representatives of all sides of industry were given responsibility for the formulation of medium-term national economic

were careful to avoid the bad relations with the T.U.C. that this lack of consultation created.

projections. From this came *Conditions Favourable to Faster Growth* and *Growth of the United Kingdom Economy to 1966*, both published early in 1963. The Labour Government used the Department of Economic Affairs, the N.E.D.C. and an Industrial Inquiry to produce *The National Plan* in September 1965; and produced a later, less ambitious document, '*The Task Ahead*' in 1969. All four documents set targets for educational expenditure.

The first chapter of *Conditions Favourable to Faster Growth* was on 'Education and Economic Growth', and stressed the dependence of economic development on a 'high and advancing level of education'.[9] The later *Growth of the United Kingdom Economy to 1966* assumed a growth rate of educational expenditure of 5.7%,[10] which was 'a considerably more rapid increase . . . than in the economy as a whole'.[11] *The National Plan* was more detailed still. Claiming to represent 'a statement of Government policy and a commitment to action by the Government', it laid out a programme for 'all education, primary, secondary, further and higher' that involved 'an increase of 32% (in expenditure) in the five year period'.[12] The future expansion of the education sector received a separate chapter in the Plan and covered the training and supply of teachers, current and capital expenditure on school buildings, and the expansion of further and higher education.

None of these documents had any major impact on economic policy; but this was not immediately clear, and the teachers' associations could not be sure in advance that these exercises in national planning would fail. Rather, they anticipated that such central determination of the distribution of national resources might set rigid limits on bargaining within the education sector, over nearly the full range of issues with which they were habitually concerned. As Sir Ronald Gould said, in December 1965,

> . . . reading the Section of the Plan dealing with education, and reading between the lines too, shows that there are many . . . vital issues which are affected, including the rate of expansion of

---

[9] N.E.D.C., *Conditions Favourable to Faster Growth* (London, H.M.S.O., 1963), p. 1.
[10] N.E.D.C., *Growth of the United Kingdom Economy to 1966* (London, H.M.S.O., 1963), p. 37, para. 205.
[11] N.E.D.C., *Conditions Favourable to Faster Growth*, op. cit. p. 1.
[12] *The National Plan* (London, H.M.S.O., 1965), p. iii and p. 179.

different sectors, teaching supply and salaries, school meals, the size of classes, and the use of training college plant.[13]

In the formulation of these documents, as in the determination of incomes policy, the teachers' associations were not consulted. There was no 'education inquiry' to match the 'industrial inquiry' that the D.E.A. launched before *The National Plan*. No one outside the Department of Education and Science asked the teachers' associations for their views on the future development of educational policy; indeed, Sir Ronald Gould publicly doubted if even 'the T.U.C. were ever asked to express an opinion on the educational section of the Plan and certainly teachers' organisations were not'. 'Teachers can fret and fume about the Plan', Sir Ronald said, but they 'have no means of shaping it.'[14] The move of the larger associations towards an alliance with organised labour corresponded precisely with the creation of the N.E.D.C., with the involvement of the T.U.C. in the machinery of national planning, and with their own exclusion from these consultative processes.

The balance of payments and educational expenditure

The significance of Government decision-making outside the education sector for the degree of influence possible to the teachers' associations within it, was the lesson that the associations took from their experience of educational growth, incomes policy and national planning in the 1960s. The new forms of behaviour that they adopted reflected this. The education cuts of January 1968 were, in this sense, a postscript for the decade; in that they reinforced an analysis already made, that the traditional forms of teacher pressure were of themselves insufficient to guarantee influence to the teachers' associations.

The underlying deficit in Britain's balance of payments in the 1960s brought recurrent payments 'crises . . . continual recourse to international borrowing (and) accumulated debt repayment obliga-

---

[13] Sir Ronald Gould, *National Planning and the Education Service* (London, College of Preceptors, 1966), p. 7. The text of a speech in December 1965.
[14] Ibid. p. 16. Nor could they gain access to the D.E.A. in 1966, even when that Department was responsible for incomes policy, and when headed by a Union sponsored M.P.

tions'.[15] A balance of payments kept in surplus in the 1950s only by favourable terms of trade gave way to a persistent deficit by 1964 which preoccupied Governments. The prime purpose of economic policy up to 1967 was to defend the parity of sterling, and thereafter, to guarantee the effectiveness of devaluation. With Governments refusing to devalue before 1967, and committed to making devaluation work after it, and with low reserves of foreign currencies throughout, the vulnerability of the balance of payments, and the international borrowing that resulted, impinged directly on policies adopted by the Department of Education and Science in the second half of the 1960s.

The significance of overseas payments crises for the policy of the D.E.S. was clear even in 1961, in that the 'pay pause' was a response to such a crisis. Equally, it was in defence of the pound, and to protect the reserves, that Governments placed a moratorium on higher education building in July 1965,[16] and set a nil norm for salary increases (including those of teachers) in July 1966. It was to guarantee the effectiveness of devaluation, and to meet the requirements of international creditors, that the Chancellor of the Exchequer cut public sector (and primarily educational) expenditure in January 1968, and later committed the Government to a limit of 3% in real terms on the growth rate of local authority expenditure (of which education is the largest single item).[17]

For what one respected education correspondent has called 'the lotus years' are clearly over.[18] An average annual rate of expansion of educational expenditure of 7% in real terms between 1945 and 1968 has been replaced by one of less than 4% in 1969/70, and

[15] S. Brittan, *Steering the Economy* (London, Secker and Warburg, 1969), p. 268.
[16] This is clear from the statement of the Chancellor in the Commons on 27 July 1965, that 'to ensure that we reach our aim of eliminating the deficit (in the balance of payments) in the course of next year, and of maintaining the strength of sterling, the Government have decided ...to slow down the rate of expenditure on capital projects...by Government Departments'. (*House of Commons Debates*, vol. 717, col. 228, 27 July 1965.) The Secretary of State for Education and Science later explained the significance of this for university building: 'In general, all university building projects planned to start since July 27th ... are subject to six months deferment.' (Ibid. vol. 718, col. 331, 28 October 1965).
[17] For details of these cuts, see Chapter 7.
[18] Brian MacArthur, *The Times*, 10 March 1970, p. 11.

the indications now are that it has dropped still further to 2% in the early 1970s. For so long as the rate of growth of the demand for education continues to exceed that of G.N.P., Government decisions on the distribution of its expenditure between public services will remain central to the attainment or non-attainment of the goals of the teachers' associations. Equally, with education as the second largest single item of Government expenditure, the Treasury's control of the size and growth of the public sector in total – a control intimately linked with its management of the economy – will bring close Treasury inspection of the total costs of policies adopted by the D.E.S. In consequence, the new forms of behaviour that the teachers' associations adopted in the 1960s to gain influence on these wider Government policies are not likely to be abandoned in the decade that follows.

NEW FORMS OF BEHAVIOUR IN THE 1960s

The new forms of behaviour adopted by the teachers' associations in the 1960s were of two kinds. They involved the adoption of new strategies, where the problem was to gain access to centres of government decision-making hitherto ignored; and they involved the adoption of new tactics, to gain greater influence within the associations' traditional strategy of concentration on the Department of Education alone. In these two ways, the associations sought influence in the formulation of wider Government policy affecting the education sector, and a greater impact on the application of such policy there.

In practice, not all the teachers' associations adopted all the new forms of behaviour – the smaller associations in particular were involved in only some. Equally, of the new forms of behaviour adopted, one (the search for organisational unity and professional self-government) owed less than the others to the changes in policy just described. Its origins lay in longer-held goals of the teachers' associations; but even here, the traditional arguments for one union and for a Teachers' General Council were reinforced by the need, recognised by the leaders of the associations, to strengthen their bargaining position before the D.E.S. in this new context of policy.

With these provisos, the new forms of behaviour adopted by organised teachers in the 1960s can be seen as a response to the changing pattern of policy just described. Teachers were subject to the results of policy made outside the education sector, in consultative processes to which their associations had no ready or regular access, and against relationships of power in which the teachers were too small to be influential alone. Even in negotiations with the D.E.S., the traditional forms of behaviour adopted by the associations could not guarantee influence – even when the associations were themselves united (which was rare). Constrained by policy made outside the education sector, and with no guarantee of influence within it, the teachers' associations adopted new *strategies* in an attempt to influence wider Government policy, and new *tactics* within the education sector to shape the implementation of Government policy there.

These new strategies and tactics took four forms. The associations attempted to strengthen their position before the D.E.S. by reviving an old tactic of *organisational unity and professional self-government*, and by adopting the new tactic of *national scale militancy*. In addition, the associations attempted to increase Government commitment to education as a policy priority in the distribution of public expenditure by creating *an alliance for educational advance*; and lastly, to gain access to decision-making on national economic policy, by forming *an alliance with organised labour*. These four reactions (the first two, tactical innovations within the associations' traditional strategy: the second two, tactical alliances occasioned by innovations in strategy by the associations) are considered in turn in the chapters that follow.

5

Organisational Unity and Professional Self-government

Both organisational unity and professional self-government were, at one and the same time, tactics revived in the 1960s and goals long held by the teachers' associations. Each was an attempt to strengthen the bargaining position of teachers before the Department of Education, by the creation of a coalition of the associations: either through the formation of a single voice for organised teachers; or through the use of a teacher-dominated council with statutorily-defined powers.

THE SEARCH FOR ORGANISATIONAL UNITY

The impetus for the creation of a single teachers' organisation has come always from the largest association, the N.U.T. For beyond the importance of unity for the status and image of the profession, the Union believed that a single voice for teachers would make it possible for the profession to make its representation felt to the full. Lack of unity, in the Union's view, dissipated the potential for influence that the teachers collectively possessed through the traditional forms of their pressure. And, of course, as the largest of the associations by far, the N.U.T. had the most to gain from the creation of an organisational unit that it would inevitably dominate, and in which sectional voices would be muted.

To these arguments for organisational unity, the N.U.T. added another in the 1960s; that as the provision of education became more expensive, and as the Government developed policies of prices and incomes, teachers should unite to meet this growing concentration of power in the hands of central Government. As one N.U.T. leader put it:

> If the administrative power in education, which was once diffused, is now being concentrated in the Minister, then the power of the teachers, which is at present diffused, should be concentrated too. We should create our own national power centre to parallel that

of the Minister... Unity then is no longer a luxury, it is becoming a necessity, for unity means political power, and disunity, political futility.[1]

When the N.U.T. approached the N.A.S. and the Joint Four in 1960, three attempts to create a single association of teachers in England and Wales had already failed. All that remained of sixty years of recurrent negotiations was the Joint Committee of the Four Secondary Associations, and a joint membership scheme between the N.U.T. and the AT.T.I.

Relations between the associations were at their worst in the 1890s, and though the Secondary Associations co-operated with the N.U.T. before 1914, they did so with the same fears of absorption by the Union that were to prevent the creation of a single teachers' organisation in the 1960s. The associations came nearest to organisational unity in 1924, when the N.U.T., Joint Four and A.T.T.I. formed a loose confederation that involved no loss of autonomy by the separate associations. This proved ineffective and collapsed in 1932; and though negotiations re-opened between the six associations in 1936, these deadlocked on the Joint Four's refusal to sink their identity in a single association. The only progress towards organisational unity that emerged from these protracted negotiations in the 1930s was a joint-membership scheme between the N.U.T. and A.T.T.I.

After the war, these two associations renewed the initiative for unity. In 1946, they invited the Joint Four and N.A.S. to discuss professional unity based on the elimination of competitive recruitment. In the negotiations that followed, neither the Joint Four nor the N.A.S. would accept the N.U.T.'s proposal for an all-embracing 'Institute of Education for England and Wales'. Nor would the N.U.T. participate in the type of confederation (of the 1924 type) that the smaller associations proposed. With their positions so clearly irreconcilable, the associations abandoned their discussions in December 1949, and did not resume them until late in the 1950s.

A call for organisational unity reappeared at the N.U.T. conference in 1956; and as a result, exploratory talks were opened with the A.T.T.I. in 1957, and with the N.A.S. and the Joint Four in 1961. Throughout these negotiations the Union maintained its hostility

---

[1] *The Teacher*, 19 April 1963, p. 5 (Sir Ronald Gould).

to any loose confederation that would leave the autonomy of the existing organisations undisturbed. It argued that such a confederation had failed in the past; and that whilst competitive recruitment remained, any such 'common council' would either be obliged to restrict its activities to that narrow range of issues on which the associations were already in agreement, or would simply provide yet another arena in which the associations could compete for members. It insisted that the only real basis for unity was the creation of a single teachers' organisation.

The new body that the N.U.T. proposed in 1961 was to have a central council, elected partly by the membership, and partly by the membership divided into sections by the type of institution in which they taught. Each section was to have its own executive committee, which would be autonomous in matters of salary negotiation and in educational topics relating to its field alone. There would be a general conference, and sectional conferences, as the supreme policy-making organs; and into this body the existing associations were to sink their identities.

The N.U.T. claimed that this constitution allowed for the separate representation (within its semi-autonomous sections) of teachers with special interests. In fact, it allowed only for the separate representation of teachers in institutions of further education. Secondary teachers were to be in the same section as primary teachers, and the Union proposed no separate sections for men teachers or for heads. If this had been accepted by the other associations, the A.T.T.I. would in effect have occupied a separate section, whilst the Joint Four, N.A.S. and N.A.H.T. would have been absorbed into a section dominated by the membership of the N.U.T. The associations' reactions to the Union's proposals followed directly, even anticipatably, from the degree of autonomy the proposed constitution offered to the membership of each.

The special position of teachers of further education within the N.U.T.'s proposed teachers' organisation reflected the impact on Union thinking of exploratory talks held with the A.T.T.I. in 1957, before the Union's proposals were themselves finalised. For from the outset, the N.U.T. recognised that the constitution of an all-embracing organisation could only rest on one of three bases. It could rest on sectional groupings that paralleled the present organisational divisions; or on the willingness of the existing associations to surrender their autonomy; or, failing both these, on a guarantee of some degree of autonomy to sectional groups within a unitary structure. The Union would not tolerate the first, nor the A.T.T.I. the second. That it was the third alternative that the N.U.T. later offered to the Joint Four and to the N.A.S. followed from the A.T.T.I.'s insistence that it would accept no scheme of unity which failed to give technical teachers complete autonomy in their own field, particularly in Further Education and in salaries.

Representatives of the two associations agreed that the only practicable basis of a unitary constitution was one allowing sectional representation to teachers by the type of educational institution in which they taught, with the main sectional division being that between 'schools' and 'institutions of further education'. They agreed that the constitution of the new body should contain certain 'entrenched clauses', safeguarding certain areas of autonomy to each sectional group. Yet even with this guarantee of autonomy, the A.T.T.I. was not prepared to proceed to unity alone. It would not join a united body unless the new organisation absorbed other teachers' associations, particularly the Joint Four. On its suggestion, the talks were adjourned to await the outcome of the N.U.T.'s approach to the other associations.

The Joint Four Secondary Associations accepted the N.U.T.'s invitation to talks in 1960, where they all rejected the Union's plan. In particular, each rejected the proposed section that would absorb all primary and secondary teachers. They argued that by it, their members would be in a minority; and the four associations would lose both their representation on national bodies like the Burnham Committee, and their right of direct and separate access to the Minister and to the local authority associations. This they found too high a price to pay for organisational unity.

Talks between the N.U.T. and the N.A.S. proved more difficult still. The two associations have had a long history of mutual recrimination and competitive recruitment since the N.A.S. broke away from the N.U.T. in 1922; and even during the discussions of 1961, neither refrained from publicly attacking the other. The N.A.S. had long been sceptical of the Union's repeated appeals for solidarity in the presentation of salary demands, and of its call for organisational unity. In each, the Association had seen attempts to undermine its autonomy and to reduce its membership; and like the Joint Four before it, the N.A.S. was not prepared to surrender the autonomy that separate organisational existence guaranteed. Anticipatably, the talks in 1961 failed. The N.A.S. rejected the proposed unitary constitution, and argued instead for a federal council, to facilitate common action when the organisations were already in agreement. The Association's only concession from its position in 1948 was to allow such a 'common council' the minimum of executive powers. This did not satisfy the N.U.T.

As with the Joint Four, all that came of these discussions was a commitment to co-operate on issues of common policy; and this was insufficient to prevent sharp exchanges between the two associations in the 1960s. When the N.U.T. approached the A.T.T.I. a second time in the wake of the N.A.S. discussions, the Association's unwillingness to change its formal relationship to the Union only reinforced the point; that the commitment of the smaller associations to their autonomy, the long-established hostility between certain of them, and the N.U.T.'s refusal to allow them all representation within a loose federal structure, had defeated yet another attempt to create a single teachers' union.

There were two postscripts to these discussions: the first, a renewed initiative for unity by the N.U.T.; the second, the temporary growth of co-operation between the associations in the second half of the 1960s.

The Union's conference in 1967 voted, in the face of executive opposition, for fresh talks with the other teachers' associations to promote 'a working partnership with the ultimate aim of achieving one united organisation within the teaching profession'.[2] The executive's response to this call was slow, but when it came it showed a marked change of approach from that adopted in the early 1960s. Instead of an attempt to form an all-embracing teachers' organisation, the Union set out to find areas of co-operation between existing associations. In June 1969, the Joint Four, the N.A.H.T. and the Association of Teachers in Colleges and Departments of Education agreed to join the N.U.T. in working parties to examine the Government's proposals on occupational pensions, and the recommendations of the Maud report on local government. Later, the invitation to participate in these working parties was extended to the N.A.S. and to the A.T.T.I.

These arrangements only formalised *ad hoc* contacts between the associations on non-controversial issues which had existed through

---

[2] *The Teacher*, 7 April 1967, p. 16.

the decade.[3] For the permanent officials of each association were, and are, in frequent telephone and personal contact, representatives attend each other's conferences, and the specialist services of the N.U.T. (such as its Legal Department) are normally available to the smaller associations when required. What was more significant than these working parties – though in the end it proved to be only temporary – was the extension of this co-operation to more controversial issues after 1967, and to the most traditionally hostile of the associations: the N.A.S. and N.U.T.

In 1967, the N.A.S. proposed, and the N.U.T. accepted, that the two associations co-operate in a campaign to end compulsory school meals supervision for assistant staff; and though the terms of the N.U.T.'s salary settlement with the local authorities in 1967 removed the need for such a joint campaign, the two associations found themselves united in defending that settlement against pressure from the local authorities and from the associations of head teachers. In 1969, the N.U.T., N.A.S. and by 1970 the A.M.A., co-operated in an interim salary demand, and in the strike action that followed. This co-operation, though in practice limited to the acceptance of the same target and to the sharing of information during the period of militancy, marked a sharp break from the polemic on salaries in which the N.A.S. and N.U.T. engaged through the rest of the decade. Indeed the co-operation proved to be only temporary and was followed by fierce organisational rivalry – and the normal exchange of abuse between the two associations in the salary campaign that followed. Ironically the decade that has seen so many attempts at unity now finds the associations more fiercely divided than ever.

PROFESSIONAL SELF-GOVERNMENT

On only one other issue did the teachers' associations co-operate in the 1960s. They worked together in the search for professional self-government. By self-government, teachers have long envisaged control over entry to the profession, in order to exclude the unqualified; control over discipline within the profession, in order to expel the unethical; and a single voice for serving teachers that would 'safeguard [their] material interests . . . and remedy or mitigate the

[3] ' "Non-controversial issues" are those on which the teachers' associations won't gain or lose a single member', as one association official said of Maud and pensions (private interview, December 1969).

defects of bureaucratic administration'.[4] In addition, and no less important for being less tangible, self-government would enhance the status of teachers and grant official recognition to teaching as a profession.

Attempts to achieve professional self-government are as old as the teachers' associations themselves. The search for a Teachers' Registration Council was of central concern to the N.U.T. as long ago as the 1900s and 1910s. But the Union's enthusiasm waned and the issue was abandoned until the N.A.H.T. called the major associations together in May 1960, to discuss the possible formation of a Teachers' General Council. The Association of Teachers in Colleges and Departments of Education attended this meeting and all that followed, with the Headmasters' Conference, the eight major associations and, before its demise, the National Union of Women Teachers. At this first meeting, the associations agreed to seek the formation of a body with executive powers over entry, standards and conduct for the profession – powers then shared between the Ministry, the universities and the Area Training Organisations. The Teachers' General Council was to control entry into the profession, including standards of entry to teacher training, to control professional discipline, and to monopolise the award of 'qualified status' to teachers.

To achieve such a body, the associations had first to formulate their own detailed proposals, and then to win these from the D.E.S. Neither stage of the exercise proved easy. It took an inordinately long time for the associations to agree amongst themselves the proposals that they were later to submit to the D.E.S. For the organisational rivalries that dogged the search for a single teachers' union slowed and endangered this search for professional government also. Not until July 1963 did they agree a definition of a 'qualified teacher' – a definition which determined the groups to be admitted to the Teachers' General Council. And not until July 1964 did they agree the proposed machinery of self-government that would enforce that definition of qualified status.

The Council the teachers wanted was to be 'broadly representative, with some non-teacher members, (and) with limited powers of co-option, but with registered teachers in the majority'. These

[4] Beatrice Webb, *English Teachers and their Professional Organisation* (special supplement to the *New Statesman*, Part 2, 2 October 1915, p. 23).

teachers were to be nominated by the existing associations. It was to have 'power to determine the qualifications necessary for registration of teachers working in primary, secondary, further and higher education', though not to regulate the number of entrants to the profession. In addition, the Teachers' General Council was to have powers 'to administer professional discipline and to keep a register, including the power to remove names from the register'; and, 'from a date to be determined, no further teachers should be appointed to schools recognised as efficient by the Secretary of State for Education and Science unless registered'.[5]

Such a Council could not be achieved without legislation, and in July 1964 the associations asked the Secretary of State to appoint an official working party. Quintin Hogg refused to commit himself, insisting that he would need time to consider the implications of the request. With a new Labour Government elected in October, the decision on a working party fell to a new Secretary of State, Anthony Crosland.

Anthony Crosland's reply to the associations' request did not come until November 1965; and it brought the first of a series of refusals from Labour Ministers. There was nothing between them, he told the associations, 'on the long-term aim of raising the status of the teaching profession', but the changes involved in the creation of a Teachers' General Council were radical, involving transfer to the proposed Council of the control over certain fundamental matters, such as standards of entry to the profession, which now rest with Government. He could not agree to such an alteration in the control of teacher supply at a time of teacher shortage. Nor, in any case, was Parliamentary time likely to be available for the legislation that the creation of a Council would require. Any working party would, therefore, be 'fruitless and in the end frustrating to all concerned'.[6]

The associations initially recognised that any attempt to persuade Anthony Crosland to change his mind would be unsuccessful. But in February 1966, they had convinced themselves that his refusal rested on a misunderstanding of their request. 'The call for him to set up a working party', they decided, 'did not imply immediate legislation or an early change in the method of control of entry into the teaching profession.' The Secretary of State had said, after all, that the long-term aim of raising the status of the profession deserved

[5] *The Head Teachers Review*, July 1966, p. 93.
[6] Ibid. pp. 93–4.

study. There seemed grounds for assuming therefore that 'he was in sympathy with the principle of [their] case'.[7]

On this assumption, the associations requested a second meeting, and sent with their request a memorandum on their deliberations to date. But the Secretary of State could see no point in a second meeting. 'It would serve no useful purpose', he told them, 'indeed it might create a dangerously false impression, to establish an official Working Party to investigate the matter further at the present time.' He felt that the associations' memorandum merely confirmed 'that the changes the associations (were) seeking would involve a transfer of controls over the fundamental matters of teacher recruitment from the Government to the proposed Council'.[8] This he could not accept; and he rejected a third request from the associations in November 1966.

All that the associations could do was launch a press and Parliamentary campaign, and to wait for a change in Government policy. But not until Edward Short became Secretary of State in April 1968 did Government policy modify. For Edward Short had been a serving teacher, and was an N.U.T. member and a Union-sponsored M.P. Only his personal commitment to improving the status of the profession opened the way to a Teachers' General Council; and this, in spite of continual opposition to any loss of Departmental powers amongst members of his permanent staff. By December 1968, Short had agreed to exploratory talks between the associations of teachers and local authorities, under the chairmanship of his Parliamentary Under-Secretary. From these talks came the proposals for a working party, with one representative from each teachers' association, to meet first in May 1969.

This working party, so long denied by Governments, was now endangered by inter-union rivalry. The N.U.T., never as committed as the other associations to a Teachers' General Council, refused to participate in the working party unless its representation there was increased. The Union argued that the smaller associations had compelled it to accept that representation on the Council would be by associations. It could not then accept on a working party a smaller representation than it would want on the Council itself. The matter was referred back to the Secretary of State; and it is a measure of his personal commitment to the formation of a Teachers' General Council that the deadlock was resolved without the working party

[7] Ibid. p. 94.   [8] Ibid. pp. 94–5.

being abandoned. It was, instead, reconstructed on Burnham Committee lines.

For the first time, the teachers' associations were negotiating with a Minister committed to the creation of a Teachers' General Council, 'and in consequence, few committees in the educational world have ever had their noses kept so firmly to the grindstone' as this working party.[9] Its report was published in March 1970. It proposed two bodies: a 'Teaching Council' for England and Wales, and a separate advisory body on the training and supply of teachers. The Teaching Council would have 40 members: 15 directly appointed by the Secretary of State, and 25 appointed on the recommendations of the major teachers' associations. Of these 25 people, 10 would be from the N.U.T., 3 from the N.A.S., one each from the Headmasters' Association and the Association of Head Mistresses, and two from each of the other Associations.[10] Registration with the Council would be compulsory for all qualified teachers in state-maintained primary and secondary schools, and ultimately (but not initially) for teachers in further education, colleges of education, direct grant and even independent schools. Registration would involve a 'once and for all' payment of £2; and the Register would be the mechanised record of teachers already maintained by the D.E.S., to which there would be limited public access.

The Council would assume responsibility for determining standards of admission and training, and administer professional discipline; though the Secretary of State would retain 'reserve powers' to overrule its recommendations, and to introduce his own regulations by the use of the affirmative resolution procedure. However, the working party recommended that he should accept the Council's recommendations on qualifications for entry to the profession, and on training, 'unless there were overwhelming reasons to the contrary'.[11]

This report, so much the product of Edward Short's own commitment to professional self-government, was with the teachers' associations for ratification when the Labour Government lost the 1970 General Election. The incoming Conservative administration took

---

[9] *The Teacher*, 31 October 1969, p. 2.
[10] I.e. from the A.A.M., A.M.A., A.T.T.I., N.A.H.T. and A.T.C.D.E.
[11] *A Teaching Council for England and Wales* (Report of the working party appointed by the Secretary of State for Education and Science) (London, H.M.S.O., 1970), p. 9.

no action on it; and in the event, the report was rejected by the N.U.T. and A.T.T.I. conferences in 1971. In spite of N.A.S. and Joint Four support for the working party's proposals, the new Secretary of State refused to act upon them without the unanimous support of the teachers' associations; and so the long negotiations on professional self-government have, for the moment at least, again come to nothing.

CONCLUSION

The N.U.T., as the major advocate of organisational unity, repeatedly argued that the creation of an all-embracing organisation of teachers was an essential prerequisite to the attainment of professional self-government. It was not alone in arguing this. Edward Short made much the same point to the N.U.T. conference in 1968. Speaking of 'the responsibilities of self-government', he told the delegates,[12]

> I do not see how a divided profession can shoulder these . . . convincingly. If you want me to use the next few years to make significant progress, the prerequisite is that the teaching profession in Britain must put its own house in order.

But organisational unity and professional self-government are related yet distinct themes of the 1960s, and unless Ministers refuse self-government to a divided profession, it is not clear that one automatically requires the other. For the functions of a Teachers' General Council and of a single teachers' union differ: the first, to control entry and qualifications for the profession, and discipline within it; the second, to negotiate salaries and conditions of service with employers, and even to protect the rights of the individual teacher against any self-governing teachers' body. Certainly, the smaller associations have been reluctant to accept the Union's equation of unity and self-government; and moves towards a Teachers' General Council progressed in the late 1960s even though the formal search for organisational unity failed, and in spite of the 'organisational bickering' that characterised the decade.

For organisational unity seems as far distant now as in 1960, and rivalry between the associations threatened even the long-sought

[12] *The Times*, 18 April 1968, p. 2.

working party on professional self-government. Though the predominantly common employment situation of teachers, and the weakness of a teachers' lobby divided against itself, are major forces for organisational co-operation, if not unity, it seems that the uneasy co-operation of the hitherto estranged N.A.S. and N.U.T. in the late 1960s will not quickly be repeated.

The slightest possibility remains that a Teachers' General Council could be created, so offering to the teachers' associations machinery through which to increase their influence over the standards of entry to, and discipline within the profession. Yet this is unlikely; and in any case the significance of this for the bargaining position of English teachers should not be overstated. The N.U.T. always recognised that a council without power to control entry had little point for the teachers' associations; and as one association's secretary said, 'the present proposals brought few gains to the profession, at least none commensurate with the energy expended on their achievement'. The profession can never be wholly self-governing whilst Parliamentary sovereignty remains; and however much the Council might wish to raise standards of entry to the profession, it can do this only if the Government is prepared to make available the extra money required to train teachers, or to attract in suitable trainees. What began as a search for control over entry to the profession ended in proposals for a strengthened advisory body with powers of discipline and registration, a compromise unacceptable to the N.U.T. at least.

The campaign for a Teachers' General Council reiterated the lessons of the campaigns discussed in Chapter 3, namely the limitations on the effectiveness of the traditional forms of teacher pressure in the face of a committed Department of Education. For a succession of Secretaries of State rejected any working party on a Professional Council, and only the fortuitous choice of Edward Short as political head of the D.E.S. turned complete failure into qualified success. His personal commitment, rather than any inevitable consequence of the teachers' pressure, explained the working party of 1969; and the associations could not shake Anthony Crosland's resolve, even though they were united. The intransigence of Crosland throws doubt therefore on the prime official argument in the N.U.T.'s search for organisational unity, namely that the teachers' associations were weak because they were divided.

Neither the creation of a Professional Council nor the formation of a single teachers' association would necessarily bring any greater influence for organised teachers either in policy-making at Cabinet level on the distribution of public expenditure, or in the formation of a national economic policy. Both organisational unity and professional self-government were tactical changes within the associations' traditional strategy of concentration on decision-making within the education sector alone;[13] and even here, as both the campaign for a dependants' pension scheme and that for a Teachers' General Council itself showed, unity could not guarantee influence. The machinery of self-government would provide only an additional channel of access to decision-making by the D.E.S. It would provide no additional sanctions (beyond any additional political weight generated by the professional status that such a Teachers' General Council might gather)[14] for the teachers' associations to use against an already committed Department; and lack of sanctions, rather than lack of channels of access, explains the low impact of the teachers' associations through the traditional forms of their pressure in the 1960s. The impact which the teachers' associations have on Government policy depends on the use to which organisational unity, co-operation or self-government are put, and this raises the issue of the relationship between militancy and a self-governing profession.

Militancy and self-government

Ministry and local authority spokesmen maintained in the late 1960s that the teachers must choose between militancy and professional self-government, between the methods of a trade union and the status of a profession. Edward Short told the N.U.T. conference in 1969,

---

[13] If professional self-government had been fully achieved, this would have been more than a tactical change within the associations' traditional strategic concern with the D.E.S.; in that issues on which the teachers' associations have habitually gone to the Department would have been settled by the teachers themselves. But since the Teachers' Council will depend on the Secretary of State for the implementation of its recommendations, it remains a further channel of access to the Department of Education; and, as such, fully within the associations' traditional strategy.

[14] E.g. It might be *marginally* more embarrassing politically for a Secretary of State to ignore the advice of the Teaching Council than it would be for him to ignore the advice of separate associations.

> There are loud even clamorous voices among you today who do not want professional status, but something akin to industrial status... If this course is pursued and you end up with a rule-book instead of a contract of service... you will, I am sure, live to regret the day.[15]

Even the radicals within the N.U.T. accepted this definition of the choice that they face. The Young Teachers' Conference in 1969 rejected any Teachers' General Council precisely because it would distract the associations from 'declaring themselves ready to act as a trade union'.[16]

But unless Secretaries of State are prepared to deny a Professional Council to associations unwilling to renounce militant tactics, the teachers face no such choice. For there is a close link between militancy and self-government, and the choice that Edward Short polarised for teachers in the 1970s obscured the possible relevance of militant action to the achievement of professional goals. Self-government for the teachers involves a limited range of issues: greater control of teacher supply, qualifications and discipline. Militancy is a tactic of far wider application; and has been used by the teachers to win what Edward Short would recognise as both 'industrial' and 'professional' goals (that is, to win greater salaries and to exclude the unqualified). Indeed, militancy may prove to be the only sanction that the teachers' associations possess both to win for their members that level of real incomes fundamental to professional status, and to increase their influence on issues over which a Professional Council has no jurisdiction (so bringing teachers nearer to a wider self-government).[17]

Certainly the 1960s saw the first attempts by the larger associations at sustained militancy on a national scale. This, more than organisational unity or professional self-government, increased their influence at key points in the decade, and set the likely pattern for the 1970s.

---

[15] *The Teacher*, 18 April 1969, p. 24.
[16] Ibid. 3 October 1969, p. 5.
[17] For a fuller discussion of the close relationship between professional and trade union goals, and of the use of militant tactics by other 'professionals', see G. S. Bain, R. D. Coates and V. Ellis, *Social Stratification and Trade Unionism* (forthcoming).

6

Militancy

English teachers have traditionally been reluctant to take strike action, but in the 1960s they resorted to militant tactics with increasing frequency and in increasing numbers. They proved willing to contemplate not simply the complete withdrawal of their labour but also the refusal to perform voluntary duties and the refusal to teach in oversize classes or alongside the unqualified. When the decade opened, the teachers' associations had never called a national stoppage; but as it closed, 100,000 teachers were on half-day and one-day strikes.

Earlier generations of organised teachers used militant tactics; but only rarely, and on a smaller scale. The first recorded strike of teachers in England and Wales occurred in Portsmouth in 1896, the second in West Ham in 1907. In 1917, strike action by teachers occurred in 32 areas, including the Rhondda, and culminated in a three-and-a-half month strike in the North Riding of Yorkshire in 1919, which closed 300 schools. Between the wars, the N.U.T. organised strikes in Southampton, Carmarthen and Abertillery, and an eleven-month strike in Lowestoft, to achieve the implementation of the national Burnham award. The N.A.S. and A.M.A. also struck in the 1920s against L.E.A.s refusing to implement Burnham agreements.

But since the Second World War, and before 1961, such militant tactics were rare. In 1951, in its dispute with the Durham County Council against the imposition of a closed-shop, the N.U.T. called on a small group of teachers to hand in their resignations, and when this conflict was renewed in 1952, the Union handed in the resignations of nearly 4,000 teachers.[1] In 1956 the Union withdrew its members from the collection of national savings, as part of its campaign against Sir David Eccles' superannuation charges; and in that same

---

[1] The N.A.S. also collected resignations from its members in May 1952. The collection of resignations enabled both associations to withdraw their members with no breach of contract, a legal nicety ignored in the 1960s.

year, selected N.A.S. members in Sunderland refused to collect school meals money.

Yet the larger associations, and eventually the A.M.A. itself, came to use militant tactics in the pursuit of policy goals in the 1960s. In 1961 both the N.U.T. and N.A.S. made calls for national and local strike action. In 1967 the N.U.T. implemented sanctions against the use of unqualified staff and the retention of teacher-supervision of school meals; and in 1969–70 the N.U.T., N.A.S. and A.M.A. called out their members in a series of strikes in pursuit of a salary claim. On each occasion, the teachers' associations drew on their detailed experience of the earlier use of militant tactics; and the successive use of such tactics indicated both the potentialities and the limitations of the strike weapon for organised teachers. It is worth considering each of these periods of militancy in turn.

THE N.A.S. AND MILITANCY

For 38 years the N.A.S. repeatedly sought representation on the Burnham Committee that negotiates teachers' salaries. At least eleven official applications and eight deputations between 1923 and 1961 failed to give the Association representation on Burnham.[2] By dint of long and diligent lobbying, the N.A.S. claim for representation was supported by a large number of back-bench Conservative M.P.s by the 1950s, but successive Tory Ministers of Education still refused the Association's demand for membership.[3] When Sir David

[2] It should be remembered that access to the machinery of salary negotiation was of major importance to the N.A.S. from its creation, for its exclusion denied the Association any participation in a major area of concern to its members. Burnham representation was also important because successive Ministers of Education limited regular consultation on a wide range of non-salary issues to associations represented there.

[3] It is worth considering briefly the reasons for this repeated rejection of the N.A.S. claim, in order to clarify the nature of the problem that the N.A.S. faced. Their later strike action was not to repeat the success of this first strike in 1961; for this alone of the examples of militancy in the 1960s was primarily an inter-union dispute. The defeated party in 1961 was not the Government but the N.U.T. Indeed, in 1960, the Union went so far as to circulate a memorandum to all M.P.s, arguing against N.A.S. representation, a day before the N.A.S. deputation to the Minister. The Government abandoned the Union only when to defend it was made politically embarrassing by the N.A.S. strike action, and only when the workings of the Burnham Committee were themselves under review.

Eccles refused yet another N.A.S. deputation in 1959 he merely followed the precedent set by his predecessors, and underlined the inadequacy of the traditional tactic hitherto adopted by the N.A.S. in its search for membership of Burnham.

Faced with yet another Government refusal, the N.A.S. extended the range of tactics it was prepared to adopt. It began a two-part campaign. The first, a continuation of its long-standing policy of Parliamentary pressure, brought 88 signatures to a Commons' motion and by early 1961 had won the support of 235 M.P.s (all but a handful of whom were on the Conservative backbenches). In addition the N.A.S. turned to more direct action. In February 1961, it held a mass rally in London, attended by 6,000 members and followed by a march down Whitehall. At its 1961 conference, delegates voted for 'militant action' to protest against N.A.S. exclusion from Burnham, the lack of an independent inquiry into teachers' salaries, and the 'gross underpayment of schoolmasters'. A series of local strikes

> The official reasons for the Association's exclusion obscure this basic fact, that the Government kept the N.A.S. out of Burnham to appease the N.U.T. If the reason given for its exclusion was 'size', the N.A.S. was still refused access when it was the second largest association. The argument used in 1951 that to give access to the N.A.S. would open the way to other associations begged the question of the validity of the Association's case. The refusal in 1957 that rested on the N.A.S.'s opposition to Government policy on 'equal pay' quietly forgot that the N.U.T. had opposed Government policy on 'equal pay' for 36 years when a member of the Committee. The argument of 1955 that only associations representing areas of education should be on the committee discriminated against any general union, and looked like a rationalisation after the decision. To argue that the Teachers' Panel without the N.A.S. either 'adequately' (1955) or 'fully' (1944) represented the teachers' interests failed to account for the rapid growth in the membership of the N.A.S., which has been, after the A.T.T.I., the fastest growing association since the war.
>
> The criteria for membership of Burnham were apparently stacked against the Association, and changed with each appeal. On this, Lord Hailsham was more candid than his predecessors. There was, he said, 'no particular criterion' for membership, and the considerations which determined membership would not 'codify at any given moment'.
>
> But the Association's use of Parliamentary pressure and deputations had rested on the assumption that criteria governing entry existed, and that the N.A.S., having met the requirements laid down, could then reason its way in. With Lord Hailsham's reply, the fallacy of the assumption was clear, and the inadequacy of the tactics adopted was demonstrated.

followed, in each of which members from a single school were withdrawn for a day.

In the autumn, the pattern of strikes altered. The Association called the first national strike of teachers in England and Wales on 20 September. More than 20,000 teachers came out for a one-day stoppage, and at least 18,000 attended protest meetings in eight regional centres and in London. It was in the wake of this strike that Sir David Eccles agreed to meet the Association and, late in October, granted them membership of Burnham.[4] On the understanding that the Association would not allow its opposition to the policy of equal pay to obstruct the working of the Committee, the Minister gave the N.A.S. two seats (it had asked for four) on the Burnham Committee that met in March 1962.

There is a postscript to this period of militancy. For by its actions in 1961, the Association earned a reputation for militancy that persisted through the 1960s; and the 9,000 extra members who joined it that year reinforced its executive's commitment to the use of such tactics. But it was not to repeat its success of 1961, though it made two further attempts. In 1965 it threatened, and in 1969 actually implemented, strike action in support of its demand for an independent inquiry into teachers' pay. But the campaign of 1965 was discreetly abandoned in the face of Government opposition; and the strike for an inquiry into teachers' salaries in 1969 ended with an inquiry into who should pay the salaries of teachers on strike – not quite the initial objective. For by the end of the 1960s, N.A.S. militancy was overshadowed by that of the N.U.T., itself the product of changes in N.U.T. tactics evident over the decade as a whole.

THE N.U.T. AND MILITANCY
'Uneasy Beginnings' 1961

The Union's abortive excursion into strike action in 1961 was an exercise in paradox and inconsistency. The Union spent the major

[4] This is not to imply any simple relationship between N.A.S. strike action and that concession of Burnham membership. Sir David Eccles was already involved in a major restructuring of the Burnham Committee when the N.A.S. called its national strike. However, without that strike action, it is hard to see why the Minister should have included the N.A.S. in his restructuring. On the report of this see R. D. Coates, 'The teachers' associations and the restructuring of Burnham'. *British Journal of Educational Science* (June 1972, pp. 192–204).

part of June, July and September committed to strike action, whilst in late August it joined other teachers' associations in denying the usefulness and relevance of the strike weapon. Moreover, the Union threatened to strike in September in order to achieve a salary settlement against whose implementation it had planned to strike in June and July. The threat of strike action was the same; the objective reversed. Indeed the Union spent part of September proposing to strike and work at the same time! Twice special conferences of the Union called for strike action at the executive's request; and twice the executive reversed these conference decisions. In the end, the Union settled, without strike action, for an agreement that met neither their requirements of July nor those of September. 'It [was] understandable', as the *Schoolmaster* said, 'that teachers [were] bewildered.'[5]

The confrontation of 1961 began when the Burnham Committee's provisional settlement of 30 May was rejected by the N.U.T. executive early in June. The Union's leadership was divided then, as throughout. Rejection was agreed only by 26 votes to 15, and the decision to recommend a token one-day national strike, and area strikes of longer duration, was carried by only one vote. These strike proposals were put to a special conference of Union delegates later in June and it is significant, in the light of what followed, that the delegates did not vote on them. They were adopted by default and narrowly at that.[6]

By the time the Burnham Committee next met on 27 July, the Chancellor of the Exchequer had already announced his 'pay pause', and Sir David Eccles had rejected both the size and the distribution of the provisional settlement. Though the Union initially pressed for a larger settlement, its executive quickly if reluctantly decided to ratify the agreement of 30 May in an attempt to defend that from the cuts demanded by the Minister. The N.U.T. leadership abandoned its plans for militancy; and both Panels of the Burnham Committee

[5] *The Schoolmaster*, 27 October 1961, p. 789.
[6] The conference voted instead on a conservative amendment to call another special conference if negotiations in the Burnham Committee failed. The amendment was carried on a show of hands, but narrowly defeated in the ensuing card vote. The special conference committed the Union to its first ever national strike, and to its first systematic area strikes for over three decades, by a majority of only 16,000 in a total vote of over 200,000. The excursion into militancy began as shakily as it was to continue.

defended the settlement against Sir David Eccles through the summer of 1961. At the end of August, the Union met the other associations of the Teachers' Panel and agreed that it would be better 'to concentrate on political action and to avoid strikes'.[7]

The Union and its leadership were almost equally divided on the question of strike action; and N.U.T. policy fluctuated with the temporary ascendance of one side or the other. So, early in September – under pressure from the militants within the Union – the N.U.T. leadership again decided to recommend strike action to a second special conference. Yet even before the conference met, the executive moderated its initial strike proposals. On 8 September, it recommended sanctions on a wider scale than those proposed in June: not only a national one-day strike and area strikes as before, but also the complete withdrawal of the services of Union members from the school meals service from 1 November. By 18 September, the moderates within the Union executive had changed this to a suggestion that the teachers should strike and work at the same time. That is, as in 1927 at Lowestoft, the teachers should resign from the service of the L.E.A. whilst seeking the authority's permission to continue teaching in the schools (so, the moderates argued, demonstrating their opposition to the Government without hurting the children). Both these sets of strike proposals were put to members in 59 areas in referenda in September, and a national referendum was held to determine support for a strike levy.

The referenda results were a major defeat for the Union militants. For only 43.7% of the Union's membership in the selected areas (though 51.4% of those voting) supported full strike action, and a tiny additional 6.1% favoured the 'strike and work' proposals of the executive. Three teachers in five in those areas selected for strike action therefore favoured strikes of some form, but this fell short of the 75% required by the executive to set such action in motion. In addition, only a half of those who voted in the national referendum (and only 37% of the total Union membership) were prepared to pay a levy to finance strike action in selected areas.

The special conference on 7 October was clearly out of sympathy with this result. Because of the referenda, delegates could no longer support area strikes, but they voted through a proposal for a one-day national strike, and the extension of the ban on school meals duties

[7] *The Schoolmaster* (in an open letter to the N.A.S.), 15 September 1961, p. 440.

to include a ban on supervision both before and after the meal. Faced with a choice between a militant special conference and a divided membership as shown in the referenda, the executive abandoned its strike plans on 16 October. In return for a Government promise to postpone legislation on the reform of the Burnham Committee, the Union agreed to implement the cuts in the May settlement demanded by Sir David Eccles.

The executive's always hesitant commitment to militant tactics required the support of more than a bare majority of those Union members who would have been called upon to implement it. The referenda demonstrated the absence of this support amongst at least 40% of those polled, just as the vacillations of the executive in September demonstrated the divisions within the Union leadership itself. But even a united leadership would have required mass support for the action proposed by the militants within the Union, and in 1961 this support was absent. Divided to the end, the executive accepted the logic of this only by 25 votes to 15; and the Union's first attempt at militancy in the 1960s was abandoned before it had begun.

The 'sanctions' campaign of 1967

The divisions in the Union in 1961, which so dogged its attempts at militancy from the outset, were not evident in the Union's 'sanctions' campaign of 1967. Here the Union sought a salary settlement in excess of that laid down as the 'norm' in the Government's prices and incomes policy, by the adoption of 'sanctions' (the refusal to supervise school meals and to work alongside unqualified teachers) which had themselves long been Union objectives. Indeed, their choice as sanctions reflected the growing impatience of Union members with the continued presence of meals duties and unqualified teachers, an impatience of longer standing than the immediate salary dispute. But the campaign itself began, even if it did not end, as a reaction by the Union to the impact on Burnham of the incomes policy adopted by the Labour Government in July 1966.

The N.U.T. conference in 1966 re-established twin salary priorities for the Union: a much improved basic scale, and the abolition of the primary–secondary differential.[8] In spite of the wage 'freeze'

[8] This refers to the lower salaries that, on average, teachers in primary school receive relative to their equivalents in secondary schools, that result partly from the artificial concentration of 'posts of responsibility' (for which extra 'above scale' salary is paid) in secondary schools.

imposed in July, the Teachers' Panel of Burnham twice attempted to open salary negotiations. On each occasion, the Management Panel refused: in November, until the Government had published its White Paper on 'the period of severe restraint'; and in February until the Government had determined guidelines for incomes in the period after July 1967. Negotiations eventually opened in April 1967 but deadlocked after two months, and went to arbitration (a move staunchly opposed by the N.U.T.).

To a special conference of the Union, the executive then proposed that, if further negotiations failed, the Union should immediately implement its policy on school meals and on unqualified teachers.[9] From the floor of the conference came further proposals for regional withdrawals of labour to be financed by a national levy on all members.[10] The goal of this 'phased series of sanctions' was initially clear: to win a salary settlement which gave a better basic scale, ended the primary–secondary differential, and safeguarded the salaries of young teachers affected by secondary reorganisation.

Unlike 1961 the executive found no shortage of volunteers to implement sanctions. Of 627 local associations of the Union, 543 were willing to withdraw from the school meals service, and 594 were willing to refuse to teach alongside the unqualified. From these, the executive chose 46 in which it held referenda on the sanction proposals. 70.2% of the membership there supported sanctions on school meals, and 69.5% on the unqualified.

The arbitrated award announced in August made only marginal changes to the original Management offer. It met the teachers' demands only on the safeguarding of salaries, and the Union, in August, decided to continue sanctions. But there was a clear shift of emphasis in the campaign. For when the executive listed the goals of sanctions early in September, the sanctions had themselves become a goal. No longer did the N.U.T. require just a much-improved basic scale and the removal of the primary–secondary differential, but also immediate action by the Government and the local education authorities to meet Union policy on school meals and unqualified persons.

[9] I.e. to end school meal duties by 1 April 1968, and 'in no circumstances [to] accept auxiliaries in the schools to perform teaching duties'.

[10] The special conference also reduced the majority required in local referenda from 75% to 66⅔%. An attempt to reduce it to 50% was defeated.

Sanctions began as planned in September, and provided the background to a long series of meetings between the Union, the local authority associations, and the new Secretary of State for Education and Science, Patrick Gordon-Walker. At the very first meeting of the Union and the Secretary of State in September, Gordon-Walker made clear his sympathy for Union policy on both school meal duties and the unqualified. But he refused to re-open the arbitrated salary settlement before the time for the next salary negotiations, 'a position from which he did not depart in the following weeks'.[11]

By the early days of November indeed, the Government, the local authorities and the N.U.T. were sufficiently close for settlement on both the question of unqualified teachers and that of compulsion in school meals duties. But on the question of salaries, and on the primary–secondary differential, the difference between the local authorities and the Union remained wide, and prevented settlement until the end of November.

The Union initially demanded that the primary–secondary differential be abolished from April 1968, and a new salary settlement implemented from September 1968. The local authorities countered early in November, with a refusal to renegotiate the salary settlement until April 1969, and the promise of a working party within the Burnham Committee, 'to examine the structural problems, primary–secondary differentials and so on'.[12] This did not satisfy the Union, who nonetheless conceded a little. It would end sanctions if the local authorities 'would look sympathetically, before the next round of Burnham negotiations, at a much improved basic scale', and if they would announce their 'plain intention to remove the primary–secondary differential from 1 April 1969.'[13] The Union thus abandoned their immediate salary demand, and conceded twelve months on the abolition of the primary–secondary differential, but even this did not bring a settlement. All the local authorities would concede by 13 November was a working party to consider the differential with no prior commitment, and this was not enough for the Union.

Local authority attitudes hardened. By 17 November, their national associations proposed that teachers pursuing sanctions after 1 December should be suspended without pay. The Union replied that if a single teacher was suspended as a result of sanctions, their

---

[11] *N.U.T. Annual Report 1968*, p. 103.
[12] Ibid. p. 105.   [13] Ibid. p. 105.

entire membership would withdraw from the school meals service. New sanction areas began on 22 November, and three days later the Union announced plans for a strike levy on its membership, and its intention to withdraw, at a date to be announced, all its members 'from non-statutory duties connected with the School Meals service'.[14] At Easington in County Durham, the local authority anticipated the authorities' policy by suspending all Union members implementing sanctions from 27 November.

The Union and the local authority associations reached an agreement as the Easington suspensions began. A form of words was agreed that committed the local authorities to a marked reduction in the primary–secondary differential. In return the N.U.T. agreed that negotiations for the next salary settlement would not begin until the autumn of 1968, to be implemented early in 1969. In addition, two working parties were to be established: one to report, if possible within a month, on how best to end the regulation compelling teachers to supervise school meals; and the other, to report within six months, on the question of the unqualified teacher.

These working parties reported in 1968. That on school meals duties reported in March, and compulsion was abolished in August. The working party on unqualified staff set 1970 as the date after which no local authority should employ temporary or occasional staff, and this was accepted by the Government. The primary–secondary differential, for whose abolition the Union had continued sanctions through November, was markedly reduced (though not abolished) by the creation of 9,000 posts of responsibility in primary schools in the 1969 salary settlement. Indeed that settlement was accepted only reluctantly by the N.U.T. largely because it contained this reduction in the differential. Its acceptance in March 1969 set the scene for the interim salary demand that followed.

THE INTERIM SALARY DEMAND OF 1969–70

When Sir Ronald Gould, as spokesman for the Teachers' Panel, accepted the Burnham settlement of March 1969, he took the unprecedented step of warning both the Government and the local authorities that they 'should take note of the serious discontent that at present is found in the teaching profession'.[15] The N.U.T., he said, had only accepted the settlement reluctantly as the best for which they

[14] Ibid. p. 108.   [15] *The Teacher*, 14 March 1969, p. 8.

could hope under the prices and incomes policy; and the N.A.S. and A.T.T.I. had rejected it completely. The discontent of which he spoke had by Easter committed both the N.A.S. and N.U.T. to an interim salary demand.

The N.A.S., at its Easter Conference, carried an executive proposal that salary negotiations re-open, with only eight of the 800 delegates voting against the resolution. The N.U.T. conference was more evenly divided, with the majority of the executive opposing any call for an interim salary increase. But the floor defeated the platform, to commit the Union to an interim pay award from 1 April 1970. To this, the initial local authority reaction was uncompromising. 'A polite letter of refusal', Sir William Alexander is reported to have said, is all that the teachers would get.[16]

On the Union's initiative, the N.A.S. and N.U.T. held talks through the summer, on the co-ordination of action in support of the salary demand; and when the strikes came in the autumn, officials of the two associations met regularly to exchange information and to co-ordinate strike activity. By June, the Union was already laying plans for strike action in the event of deadlock; and in a salary publicity campaign begun immediately after Easter, issued 30,000 posters and 40,000 handbills before the summer vacation.[17] By July, the A.M.A. had also announced its support for an interim increase; and in September, all the associations on the Teachers' Panel of the Burnham Committee agreed to a united demand for a flat rate increase of £135 per teacher from 1 April 1970 – an 8% demand costing £44m., that was put to the Management Panel of Burnham in October.

In the negotiations that followed, the confrontation escalated with each meeting of the Burnham Committee; but teachers had already struck, and held mass rallies, before the Committee first met. In July 7,000 London teachers struck for half a day, to march through the capital in support of their demand; and on the initiative of the N.U.T. executive mass rallies and protest marches were held by local associations throughout the country in September and October.

---

[16] The Secretary of the Association of Education Committees, quoted in the *Times Educational Supplement*, 9 May 1969, p. 1534.
[17] The whole campaign saw a major publicity drive, which included page-long advertisements in *The Times* and *Guardian* of 6 October; and one million posters and leaflets issued by the N.U.T. in the first two-week strike in December alone.

The discontent of which Sir Ronald had earlier warned was therefore already evident and organised by the time that the Management Panel replied to the teachers' demand on 10 November, when their 'derisory offer'[18] of £50 sparked off a wave of strike action at local level that the national leaderships of the associations could not have prevented even if they had so wished.[19] Over the next four weeks, over 100,000 teachers were involved in locally organised and locally led half-day and one-day stoppages; and whilst on strike, these teachers held protest marches and rallies. At the height of these strikes, on 21 November and 25 November, there were at least 25,000 teachers out of school on each day – including, on the 21st, 10,000 in London, who marched behind the N.U.T. President from the Albert Hall to Speakers' Corner.

The Union's journal remarked that this 'upsurge of spontaneous militancy [had] taken the authorities and the public by surprise'[20] and so it had. But the associations' leaders were themselves taken aback by the intensity of feeling demonstrated, and throughout the dispute that followed, their freedom of negotiation was constrained by this mass activism. Immediately after the Burnham Committee meeting, the N.U.T. executive decided both to give official support to half-day and one-day stoppages, and to hold fortnight strikes in selected schools even before negotiations on the Committee formally deadlocked.

For as they recognised, 'the impatience of Union members throughout the country [would] not wait upon long drawn-out delaying tactics by the Management Panel'.[21] But even the executive underestimated the degree of rank and file support for strike action. They initially planned to withdraw 1,000 teachers for two weeks from 1 December. In the event, 50,000 teachers volunteered, and

---

[18] Labelled this by *The Teacher*, 14 November 1969, p. 1.
[19] Even the Joint Four Associations, who recommended their members not to strike in November, recognised that certain of them would, and accordingly announced their willingness to support any teacher victimised as a result of unofficial strike action. The N.A.H.T. played no part in the strike action, leaving it to individual members to decide their own attitude to militancy. The A.T.T.I. called on all its members to strike if the local association of the N.U.T. called a half-day or one-day token stoppage, and at least 200 colleges were closed, or saw their staffs substantially reduced, as a result.
[20] *The Teacher*, 5 December 1969, p. 1.
[21] Ibid. 14 November 1969, p. 1.

the Union, allotting £250,000 for strike action, called out 4,000 teachers in 250 selected schools. In this first fortnight strike early in December, they were joined by 500 N.A.S. members in the Home Counties, and by twenty-three members of the Union of Women Teachers.[22]

The Burnham Committee reassembled on 15 December against this background of widespread strike action; and the impact of militancy could be seen in the offer then made. Only days before, the Government had announced a new incomes policy norm of $4\frac{1}{2}\%$ for 1970; and the new offer was as high as this ceiling would allow. Sir William Alexander's 'polite letter of refusal' in April, which had changed to £50 by November, was a month later replaced by a 'final offer' of £100 to every teacher earning less than £1,000, falling to an increase of £60 for those earning more than £1,525. These were increases of 11% at the bottom of the basic scale, and of $3\frac{1}{2}\%$ at the top, and overall a $4\frac{1}{2}\%$ salary increase costing £24m. The Teachers' Panel rejected this unanimously. They refused to be constrained by a $4\frac{1}{2}\%$ limit that did not apply to other wage settlements, and they would not go to arbitration so long as that was itself subject to the dictates of the prices and incomes policy.[23]

The Management Panel's two offers in 1969 were rejected by the teachers largely because of the pattern of salary settlements elsewhere. Just as the 15% increase given to airline pilots within three weeks of the Burnham settlement in March had angered teachers at their Easter conferences, so later in the year public sector wage settlements of 16% to dustmen, 12% to firemen and 10% to miners

---

[22] The N.A.S. strategy in this first set of strikes was to take out members from schools with a high percentage of working mothers, in an attempt to disrupt local industry, thereby giving the strike an 'economic sanction'. There is no evidence that this was any more effective than a random selection of schools.

[23] The two panels were clearly deadlocked on 15 December, but the Secretary of State was keen to prevent a breakdown of negotiations, and the chairman used the recent White Paper on incomes policy in 1970 as a justification for a postponement of the Burnham Committee until January. From December on, the Management Panel was publicly divided, with both the Secretary of State and the local authorities attempting to blame the other for the Management's failure to meet the teachers' demand. In fact, as the Cabinet Committee meeting under the Chancellor of the Exchequer would suggest (see p. 74) it was Treasury policy which kept the offer down.

left them unwilling to accept either a 3½% or a 4½% norm.[24] All these public sector wage settlements had been arrived at in the face of strikes, or threats of strikes, and were taken by the teachers as proof both that the Government was discriminating against them by adhering to the prices and incomes policy in Burnham, and that reasoned argument would not itself suffice to win the interim award.

This at least was the lesson drawn in December by the hitherto non-militant Assistant Masters' Association. As late as 19 November, in a letter to *The Times*, officers of the Joint Four Secondary Associations (of which the A.M.A. is one) made a public plea for a negotiated settlement without strike action. But the Association's 'profound dissatisfaction and deep disgust' with the Management offer in December led it 'to reconsider [its] attitudes towards militant action'.[25] At its Council meeting in January, the delegates were nearly unanimous in support of strikes alongside the N.U.T. and N.A.S. Only 30 of the 320 delegates voted against the motion on strike action; and in a later referendum of the entire A.M.A. membership, 62% were prepared to strike for the interim demand, and 66% to strike in 1971 at the time of the next full Burnham negotiations.

Even the Association of Assistant Mistresses, hitherto a bastion of non-militancy, held a referendum on strike action after the Burnham Committee meeting on 15 December; and found that as many as half the members who replied were prepared to support militancy as part of the major review of salaries due in 1971. Virtually all the Assistant Mistresses backed the interim demand, 75% were prepared to give half a day's salary in support of a publicity drive, and 36% were willing to strike for half a day in the current dispute.

In the New Year, the Burnham Committee met once in January and twice in February, before finally reaching a settlement early in March. The January meeting followed a Cabinet Committee chaired by the Chancellor of the Exchequer, which, according to *The Times* correspondent, authorised an extra £3.5m for the teachers.[26]

[24] Teachers' leaders, journals and letters made much of these increases, both to demonstrate the moderate nature of the teachers' demand, and the efficacy of the strike weapon.
[25] *The Teacher*, 20 December 1969, p. 8.
[26] In addition to a major salary increase for nurses. Of course, no statement came from this Cabinet Committee, but it appears that the nurses' and teachers' pay claims were high on the agenda (see *The Times*, 3 January 1970, p. 1). Certainly, an unplanned meeting of the

The resulting offer was of £100 for those earning less than £1,000 falling to £80 for those on more than £1,285. Again, this was rejected by the Teachers' Panel.

The rest of the month was spent in fruitless meetings between Senior Cabinet Ministers (Mrs Castle of the D.E.P. and Mr Short of the D.E.S.) and the teachers' associations, in a Government attempt to persuade the teachers to go to arbitration. But the teachers' associations were unconvinced, and wanted negotiated in the Burnham Committee what the Government 'hinted' they would accept only from arbitration.

The next two meetings of the Burnham Committee, both in February, brought no further increase in the interim pay award offered. On 6 February, the Management Panel repeated the January offer, with the additional proposal that a major review of salary, due to be implemented from April 1971, should be brought forward by three months. On 13 February, they proposed abandoning the interim award completely, in order to use all the money that the Teachers' Panel were demanding as part of a major review of salaries from October 1970. The Teachers' Panel accepted neither of these proposals, and the strikes went on.

After the December meeting of the Burnham Committee, the N.U.T. executive imposed a compulsory levy of £1 per month on all its members, and announced a second wave of two-week strikes in January. 4,873 teachers in 355 schools came out on 12 January; and 6,380 on 27 January. At the same time, the N.A.S. brought out 500 members each week in five selected areas in turn; and the N.U.T. held a referendum of 116,000 of its members, to select areas to be brought out in strikes of unlimited length later in February.[27] The response of this referendum was indicative of the continuing degree of rank and file willingness to strike, and therefore of the constraints on any leadership considering a settlement well below £135. 80% of the teachers polled volunteered for extended strike action; and 7,000 teachers in three areas – Birmingham, Waltham

> Management Panel was called hurriedly after the Cabinet Committee meeting, the Management Panel's 'final offer' of December increased by £3.5m. in January, and the local authorities made known that the size of this offer was dictated by the Government.

[27] Of the local associations of the N.U.T. 550 asked to be part of this referendum (i.e. at least 80% of all local associations wanted to be polled). In the event, the executive held the referendum in 230 local areas.

Forest and Southwark, began a strike of indefinite length in the week of 18–25 February. The N.A.S. supported this action by 'works-to-contract' in 48 L.E.A. areas, and also planned to bring out teachers in Manchester and the North-West connurbation from 4 March. The A.M.A. called out small numbers of its members in the three areas chosen by the N.U.T.

One further set of sanctions was planned. The N.U.T. executive made the unprecedented proposal, late in February, that in the summer term its members would refuse to inviglate G.C.E. and C.S.E. examinations. In this, they had the support of the N.A.S. who were proposing a nation-wide 'work-to-contract' in addition. The N.U.T. increased the monthly levy to as high as £6 for teachers earning more than £2,250, and organised a 'national day of protest' to coincide with the next meeting of the Burnham Committee on 3 March. This was to take the form of a national lobby of M.P.s by two train-loads of Birmingham teachers, by striking London teachers, and by deputations from each other local association of the N.U.T.

The Birmingham teachers arrived in London to find the dispute settled. In a day-long meeting of the Burnham Committee, and after personal interventions by the Secretary of State, the teachers' associations won nearly all for which they had initially asked. They received an interim pay award of £120 from 1 April 1970, and a full Burnham agreement to be negotiated in time for implementation from 1 January 1971. The strike action of 1969–70 was over, but the apparent vindication of militancy that it provided will doubtless be felt into the 1970s.

TEACHER MILITANCY IN THE 1960s
A CONCLUSION

The single most outstanding feature of these incidents of militant action through the 1960s is the growing willingness of teachers to strike. In 1961, only 37% of the N.U.T. membership were prepared even to pay a levy to finance strike action in selected areas; and 40% of those polled were unwilling to volunteer for such action. The referenda of the late 1960s mark the change. In 1967, over 500 local associations of the N.U.T. volunteered for sanctions, and more than two-thirds of teachers in selected areas were willing to implement them. This possibly reflected more a concern with the specific sanctions than with militancy itself, but by 1969 the issue was no longer in doubt. Over 100,000 teachers were involved in half-day and one-day stoppages, and the N.U.T. found more than 50,000 volunteers for its first two-week strike in December alone. The 1970 referenda only reinforced the point. Eighty per cent of Union members polled were prepared to take strike action of indefinite length, and even in the Joint Four 66% of the A.M.A. and 50% of the A.A.M. were prepared to strike in 1971. By 1970, militant tactics were established, as they had not been a decade earlier, as one option open to the associations' executives in salary negotiations. Indeed, in the interim salary demand, an initially reluctant N.U.T. leadership had little choice but to lead a strike it could not prevent. For the N.U.T. at least, the constraint on leadership imposed in 1961 by a non-militant membership was replaced in 1969–70 by the constraints of a fully militant one.

Yet militancy brought no guarantee of influence to the teachers' associations. The success of the strike action of 1969–70 was the exception for the decade, and not the rule. Even the N.A.S. strike of 1961 failed to bring the Association the number of representatives on the Burnham Committee for which it asked; and the 'victory' was more important for its effect on the Association's standing in the whole structure of advisory committees surrounding the Department than for any increase in its impact on the determination of salaries. Impotent here for want of representation before 1961, the Association remained so after 1961, trapped by the procedural conventions of a Teachers' Panel still dominated by the N.U.T.

Thereafter, N.A.S. militancy was less successful still. In 1965 and in 1969, its demand for an independent inquiry into teachers' salaries petered out in the face of Government intransigence. For the N.A.S. on each occasion faced the united opposition of the Minister and the Departmental interest groups, including the other teachers' associations; and, isolated, lacked the numerical strength to do more than marginally embarrass the Government. Only when as in 1961, its militancy was allied to substantial support amongst Government backbench M.P.s, on an issue with no significance even for Government education policy,[28] did the N.A.S. experience success by militant action. This early success led the Association to over-estimate the potency of its militancy. More normally, as in 1965 and 1969,

[28] The fight for access to Burnham was an inter-union dispute, with the Government as the reluctant arbiter.

the N.A.S. was constrained by its relative lack of numbers in an 'industry' whose organisation gives no bargaining advantage to key placed minorities,[29] and where, in consequence, size is a precondition for the impact of militancy. And of the teachers' associations, the N.U.T. alone has size.

Yet size alone brought only qualified success to the N.U.T. in 1967, and no success at all in 1961. For in common with the N.A.S. strike in 1961, each of these campaigns began, or became, attempts to improve the salary position of teachers at times when the Government, faced with overseas payments crises, were publicly committed to wage restraint. Failing to shift Governments trapped by the wider power relationships of national economic policy, the Association and the Union in each case struck a bargain that had significance within the education sector alone; settlements that had no significance for, and consequently did not call into play, the wider national and international relationships of power constraining national economic policy. On each occasion, the teachers' associations abandoned a conflict on salaries to settle for a compromise that had significance only for teachers.

In each case, this can be seen in the shifting emphasis placed on goals within the campaigns, and by the lack of congruence between initial purpose and final settlement. In 1961, the N.U.T. set out to improve a Burnham settlement of £47.5m. It settled for an agreement £5m. smaller, and a promise to delay legislation on the Burnham Committee. The N.A.S. struck in September 1961 to obtain an independent inquiry into the salary negotiating machinery, to protest against 'the gross underpayment of schoolmasters' and to win its way into Burnham. It settled for membership of Burnham alone. And in 1967, the N.U.T. planned sanctions to win an improved basic scale and an abolition of the primary–secondary differential. Yet before sanctions had been implemented, they had become themselves an objective of the exercise, and the settlement, when it came, made no concession to teachers on the basic scale.

In this respect, the interim salary demand of 1969–70 marks a sharp break with the pattern of the decade. The teachers' associations struck for a salary demand and won a salary award, with no settlement outside their initial goal; and the Government's repeated concessions (at successive Burnham Committee meetings) to ever growing militancy were a measure of that militancy's effectiveness.

[29] With the possible exception of head teachers.

The associations involved rightly took the 1970 settlement as a major victory, and as a vindication of their militancy. Yet it is not clear if this success need always be repeated. In 1969–70 the Government's incomes policy had already been broken by settlements in both the private and the public sector before the teachers struck. A General Election was looming, which the Government were uncertain of winning; and the international payments crises which had led to limitations on public expenditure in 1968 had by 1970 been replaced by a sizeable surplus on the balance of payments. It is far from certain that, if the situation had been otherwise, the teachers would have won so large an increase. Indeed given the situation, it is possibly ominous for the future effectiveness of strike action that the Government held out for so long.

For two problems remain with militancy as a tactic for organised teachers. The first concerns its effectiveness; the second, its repercussions on other goals of the teachers' associations.

Strikes by teachers are a political, rather than an economic sanction. Their power to coerce rests not on an ability to attack the financial viability of a business unit by the disruption of its productive process, which in private industry can be so successful in capital intensive industries with extended production lines, and in those facing competitive product markets with full order books. Education is not an industry of this kind. Its productive unit is small and labour intensive (the classroom and school). Its supplier is a virtual monopolist (there is a small, but Government-regulated private sector), one unconstrained at the margin by the need to maximise profits. Indeed, when teachers strike, local authorities actually save the money they would otherwise pay out as salaries to the striking teachers.

Rather, teachers strike to bring political pressure on their democratically elected employers. The disruption of the education of the child is the major asset of the teachers' strike, with the publicity it generates and the commitment and unrest that it demonstrates within the profession as secondary and important resources. The effectiveness of militancy therefore depends on the potency of other political factors limiting or strengthening the Government's will to resist; on the electoral strength of the Government, on the state of the economy, on the significance of the issues involved for Government education policy, and on the degree of public support that the teachers can attract and organise. There is no one-to-one relationship between militancy and effectiveness.

To a degree, the impact of strike action will be affected by the form that militancy takes. Refusals to undertake voluntary activities were always token gestures, disturbing the education of not a single child. The only exception to this – the ban on school meal duties – is no longer available to the teachers' associations after the settlement of 1967. Withdrawals of labour too, as has been said, have no immediate economic impact on the teachers' employers; and so long as teachers strike on full pay, there are limits to how long and in what numbers the associations can sustain striking teachers. The associations have yet to try what they only threatened in 1970 – namely a refusal to invigilate public examinations. This at least would mobilise the parents, if French experience is a guide,[30] but as yet this militant tactic has two drawbacks. It can only be used in the summer term, and there is no guarantee of conflicts occurring only then; and there is evidence – for example, in the A.M.A. referendum in 1970 – that teachers now willing to withdraw their labour totally have greater moral qualms about the use of this sanction, which singles out only certain pupils for inconvenience and hardship.

But beyond such tactical considerations of the type of strike action that would be most effective, there remains the wider problem of the impact of militancy on the full range of goals pursued by the teachers' associations. For to adopt militant tactics on an issue such as salaries within a constant set of Government public expenditure priorities, even if successful, may only redistribute expenditure within the education sector, away from those parts of the education programme on which the teachers do not strike towards those on which they do. That is, militancy alone, without a campaign to increase the flow of resources entering the education sector, may bring teachers salary increases only at the expense of other parts of their educational programme.

To capture a greater share of available resources needs more than militancy alone. As the next two chapters show, it needs action aimed beyond the Department of Education and Science, within alliances that transcend the boundaries of the education sector. The teachers' associations recognised this limitation on militancy in the 1960s and adopted strategies and tactical alliances aimed at influencing the total flow of resources entering the education sector.

[30] See J. M. Clark, *Teachers and Politics in France* (New York, Syracuse University Press, 1967), p. 110.

7

The Alliance for Educational Advance

The goals of the teachers' associations invariably involve the spending of public money, on such items as schools, equipment, training, salaries and pensions; and the ability of the Department of Education and Science to respond to those demands is ultimately limited by the availability of resources for educational provision. Indeed, in an economic situation such as Britain's in the 1960s, where the rate of economic growth did not keep pace with the growth rate of the school population, even the maintenance of prevailing educational standards, not to mention educational advance, required that the D.E.S. capture a growing proportion of available resources.

There were only three general ways in which the Department could do this: either by capturing an even greater share of total public expenditure; or by retaining a fixed share of public expenditure as total Government activity itself absorbed (by taxation and by borrowing) an ever greater share of the Gross National Product; or by a mixture of the two. The first involved the Department of Education and Science in competition with the political heads of other spending Departments; the second in a running battle with the Treasury – traditional guardian of the level of total public expenditure. In each case, the resulting level of educational expenditure was both the product and the manifestation of a political decision, on the degree of priority to be attached to education as an area of Government activity.

Traditionally, the teachers' associations have relied on a strong Secretary of State to compete for resources both with other Government Departments and with the Treasury. As Sir Ronald Gould told Anthony Crosland as recently as 1966, the associations judge the success of a Minister by 'how much money he wrings from the Treasury'.[1] But in the 1960s they attempted to achieve a more direct influence on the level of educational expenditure. In the next chapter, we will consider how the associations, by allying with organised

---

[1] *The Teacher*, 15 April 1966. (This drew from Crosland the reply quoted later that on the contrary what mattered was how much he won in competition with his Cabinet colleagues.)

labour, sought access to Treasury decision-making on national economic policy. In this chapter we will concentrate on attempts by organised teachers to strengthen the hand of the Secretary of State in bargaining with his Cabinet colleagues on the share of public expenditure going to education. They did this by forming an alliance of educationally-minded interest groups, in order to create such a level of demand for education in the electorate as a whole that Government expenditure would move in favour of education in response to democratic electoral pressures.[2]

A number of Ministers have appealed to the teachers' associations for this sort of assistance in negotiations with Cabinet colleagues. Sir David Eccles told the N.U.T. in 1961 that

> We do our cause no good if we appear to assume that we have a prescriptive right to more and more public money. We have no such right...We must justify the demands we make upon the Exchequer and the rates...I hope therefore you will constantly seek to convince the public that we want more money to enable us to give their children the best possible start in life.[3]

A similar call for a campaign to mould public opinion in favour of educational advance came from a later Secretary of State, Anthony Crosland. Replying to Sir Ronald Gould's assertion, quoted earlier,[4] he told the N.U.T.,

> With respect, this is not the point: it is how much money he wrings from the Cabinet as compared with his colleagues, the Ministers of Housing, Pensions, Health, etc. And when the Cabinet comes to decide these priorities, they try to do so first of

---

[2] The associations' traditional reliance on M.P.s was not sufficient to this task. As a recent observer of Parliament has recorded, the Commons, 'cannot easily find the occasion to debate the relative priorities of expenditure within a given total, the total itself, or the long-term implications for the economy of preferring expenditure in one sector of public activity to expenditure in another', R. Butt, *The Power of Parliament* (London, Constable, 2nd ed. 1969), p. 392. Indeed, Butt makes a strong plea for 'fuller Parliamentary debate of Government spending plans' (p. 396). The Labour Government drew up a paper, around which such a debate was held, in 1969.

[3] *The Schoolmaster*, 29 April 1960, p. 1138.

[4] Supra, p. 80.

all on merit; but they also, since we live in a democracy, take
account of popular desires. And here I must be frank with you...
what have you done to create an irresistible public demand for
more educational spending?...If you ask me for more money
you for your part must give me a stronger hand to play with.[5]

Anthony Crosland's accusation of N.U.T. inactivity here was
unwarranted. All the teachers' associations, and especially the Union,
maintain a persistent pressure on the electorate through the mass
media. In 1942, the N.U.T. had allied with the T.U.C. and the
W.E.A. in a Council for Educational Advance; and (more damn-
ing still of Crosland's accusation) all the associations had participated
in 1963 in a major, year-long publicity drive for educational expansion, the 1963 Campaign For Education.[6]

[5] *The Teacher*, 15 April 1966, p. 1.
[6] An alternative route through which to move Government spending
priorities in favour of education would be by direct affiliation to a
political party, or at least by pressure to reduce Government expenditure elsewhere by, say, policy statements on defence expenditure. The
associations have traditionally avoided both. In line with the personal
preferences of normally the majority of their executives, the associations have found strong organisational reasons for retaining their
position of political neutrality. Their need to maintain cordial relationships with all Governments regardless of party, the fear that political
alignment would cause large membership defections, and their lack
of sanctions (and therefore, to large measure, possible influence) over
Government Departments other than the D.E.S. have repeatedly led
the associations to oppose moves to align with political parties or to
publicly commit themselves on politically controversial issues arising
from Government activity in other (non-educational) sectors.

The executives have normally strictly limited the area of debate and
policy to issues determined within the education sector alone, or to
others with clear and immediate educational implications. The
boundary line has never been automatic (it is in essence arbitrary) but
by and large the associations have accepted as constraints on the range
of their dialogue the dictates of the Government's own division of
functions between its Departments. This had been challenged systematically only by the organised Left within the N.U.T. (over Suez
and the bomb in the 1950s) and with little success until the late 1960s
when both the N.U.T. and A.T.T.I. conferences passed resolutions
critical of the level of defence expenditure. Otherwise, 'politics' have
started where the education sector ends, and have been ignored by
the teachers' associations. For the very different attitude to politics
of French teachers, see J. M. Clark, *Teachers and Politics in France*

THE 1963 CAMPAIGN FOR EDUCATION

There were a number of reasons for the formation of this Campaign in 1963. N.U.T. conferences in 1961 and 1962 had demanded a greater percentage of public expenditure for educational provision, and had urged the Union to campaign for educational advance. The time was propitious. A General Election was looming, which the Government was unsure of winning; and a number of major educational reports were pending (both the Newsom and the Robbins reports were expected in 1963)[7] on which leading educationalists wished to see more Government action than on such reports in the past. There was also leadership. The initiative for the Campaign came from one man, Fred Jarvis, then Secretary of the Publicity and Public Relations Department of the N.U.T. The Campaign was his idea, which he organised and inspired with his drive and enthusiasm throughout.

In July 1962, the N.U.T. invited more than fifty educational bodies, and organisations interested in education, to discuss a possible educational campaign. At this first meeting in July, and at later meetings in 1962, the Union found a large degree of support for an educational campaign from the associations of teachers, industrial workers, education and welfare workers, church bodies and women's organisations that attended. From these meetings emerged the detailed aims and structure of what became the 1963 Campaign For Education.

The prime aim of this year-long publicity drive was 'to win public support and secure public action for a general advance in education'; and through its local activity to bring local parents into closer contact with the work and problems of the schools. The Campaign took three specific targets as the key to the general educational advance that it sought: the spending of more money, an increased supply of teachers, and the expansion of higher education without which that supply could not be provided. The winning of a larger share of public sector expenditure for education (to make education

(New York, Syracuse University Press, 1967), *passim*. See also M. Harrison, *Trade Unions and the Labour Party since 1945* (London, Allen and Unwin, 1960), Chapter 8: 'The Non-Political Unions'.

[7] The Newsom Report, 'Half our Future', on the education of the child of average or less than average ability; and the Robbins Report on 'Higher Education'.

the first expenditure priority of Government) was the Campaign's primary target, 'since no advance [could] be expected without it'.[8]

The Campaign was initially supported by 54 bodies and eventually by 86, with nine others giving sympathetic support as 'observers'. The 86 included all the major teachers' associations, with a number of church organisations, educational bodies, trade unions and civic groups. More than half the associations supporting the Campaign were educational bodies; and the rest, almost entirely trade unions or civic (predominantly women's) organisations. In addition, more than 100 distinguished people in the academic, business and public worlds accepted invitations to be its patrons.

The Campaign opened with a January manifesto and a large rally in the Central Hall, Westminster, attended by 3,000 people. This was followed by a series of public meetings in nine provincial centres between January and March. Attendance at these varied, with 1,150 at Bristol but only 500 at Cambridge. Press and television coverage was consistently high. Through the year, the national committee issued booklets, speakers' notes, films, a survey of the school building programme, and a mobile exhibition; and in June held a series of much publicised public meetings attended by many leading public figures, and addressed by the leaders of the three major political parties, supported by their educational spokesmen. And in the aftermath of the publication of the reports of both the Robbins and the Newsom committees, leading members of each committee addressed public meetings organised by the Campaign For Education.

It had always been the intention of the organisers that the bulk of the Campaign should be carried out at local level, though when this local activity began in earnest in March, only 80 local co-ordinating committees were in existence. Over the year local activity was nationwide, but its incidence was uneven and its range varied. Even so, throughout the country between March and November, local co-ordinating committees held nearly 300 public meetings, and organised brains trusts, film meetings, study conferences, exhibitions, displays, and school open days.

This local activity came to its peak in the country's first 'National Education Week' in November; and the Campaign ended with a mass rally of 5,000 people in the Albert Hall in November, amid an accolade of support from leading politicians – with leaders of all

[8] *The Schoolmaster*, 2 November 1962, p. 12.

three parties competing to give the greatest praise to the Campaign and to promise the greatest priority to educational advance.

THE COUNCIL FOR EDUCATIONAL ADVANCE

Amongst the intentions of the sponsors of the 1963 Campaign was a desire for their activity to coincide with the publication of the long-awaited Robbins Report on Higher Education, and with the General Election expected all through 1963. But the Robbins Report was delayed, and there was no General Election until October 1964. For both these reasons, and because of a reluctance to abandon so wide an alliance, the 1963 Campaign For Education continued in 1964 as the Council for Educational Advance. By early 1965, this new council was supported by 71 organisations from a field as wide as that represented by the bodies that had supported the 1963 Campaign.

The new body had a wider function than the Campaign For Education. Like the Campaign, it pressed for educational advance, and intended to promote National Education Weeks. But it was also (and indeed, these were listed first in its official functions)[9] to co-ordinate national-level activity by its member associations, to provide a forum for the discussion of educational issues, and to act as a clearing house for the exchange of information. It was also to 'police' the promises made by the political parties on the total and detail of educational advance.

The level of activity adopted by the Council was lower than that of the Campaign. Local activity was minimal, and so there were no more National Education Weeks. The finance available to the Council was less than in 1963; the local associations proved unwilling to give as much effort (often none at all) to the Council as they had to the Campaign. Activity increasingly differed in kind too. The Council began, as the Campaign had ended, preoccupied with the impending General Election; but with the election over, such publicity activity aimed specifically at the political parties gave way in importance to two other forms of activity that reflected the absence of mass local support: deputations and conferences.

The Council regularly sent deputations, letters and memoranda

---

[9] *C.E.A.: Aims and Organisation*, p. 2.

to the Secretary of State and his Ministers. It also organised conferences on specific educational issues. In addition, the Council wrote on occasion to MPs, commissioned research on teacher shortage, issued newsletters, and in 1964 published a school building survey. It was symptomatic of the differences between the Council and the 1963 Campaign that, largely for financial reasons, the Council decided against a mass rally of the 1963 kind as a means of commemorating the centenary of state education in 1970. It commissioned a booklet instead.

Unlike the 1963 Campaign, the Council by 1970 was indistinguishable from the large number of other educational bodies surrounding the D.E.S., and it had resorted to an almost total reliance on the traditional forms of teacher pressure – the deputation, the memoranda, and the occasional use of M.P.s – which were subject to all the limitations discussed earlier.[10] In particular, they were singularly inappropriate as a means of influencing decision-making outside the education sector (on, for example, the percentage of public expenditure going to education) or of defending educational expenditure at a time of retrenchment in national economic policy. These limitations were clearest at the time of the education 'cuts' of 1968, and it is worth considering the role of the Council here in detail.

When the Labour Government devalued sterling in November 1967, they deflated initially by cutting public expenditure, and only later (in the 1968 Budget) by restricting private consumption. The cuts in public expenditure came in January 1968, and fell most heavily on education. £100m. was taken off the education bill for the following two-year period; and in addition, and still more ominous for the rate of growth of educational provision, the Prime Minister announced restrictions on the rate of increase of local authority expenditure that would inevitably restrain spending on education.

The Secretary of State for Education and Science made clear the implications of this for educational expenditure. Education would no longer receive a growing share of the Gross National Product. All that Patrick Gordon-Walker could anticipate was that 'education [would] at least keep in step with the expected growth in Gross National Product'.[11] It appeared that the unprecedented growth of education since 1955, that had brought a greater share of available resources to education each year, was finally over.

[10] Supra, pp. 29–36   [11] *The Teacher*, 19 January 1968, p. 1

Against this, the Council for Educational Advance could do little. In December 1967, it joined the other teachers' associations and educational bodies in publicly insisting that education should escape the cuts; and when this did not come about, it denounced the resulting postponement of the raising of the school leaving age as 'a bitter disappointment', and, at its later Annual General Meeting, passed a motion highly critical of Government policy. But all that the Council could do in addition, beyond exchanging and publicising a series of letters with the Secretary of State on the exact meaning of the 3% limit on local authority expenditure, was to 'appeal to all affiliated organisations to maintain the utmost vigilance on this matter'.[12] But 'this matter' was nothing less than the availability of money for educational advance, which the 1963 Campaign and the Council itself had been created to win. To leave pressure on this central issue to its affiliated associations in 1968 was an indication of how far the Council had come from the days of the 'educational crusade' of 1963.

THE IMPACT OF THE CAMPAIGN AND THE COUNCIL

Even so, it is not easy to assess the impact of either the Campaign or the Council. Even in situations of apparent failure, as in 1968, it is always possible that the education cuts would have been greater but for the public outcry of the educational bodies of which the Council was one. Certainly it seems likely that the raising of the school leaving age might have been postponed for longer but for this pressure.

It seems fair to conclude that the Campaign For Education had a major impact on the political *dialogue* of the period. Education was a major issue in the 1964 Election, and though the Conservative's long-standing commitment to further and higher education, and the Labour Party's controversial proposals on secondary reorganisation, would probably have made education an election issue anyway, the Campaign and the early Council maintained pressure on the politicians in the long run-up to a closely fought election.

Yet as the Campaign itself recognised, 'what eventually counts most in assessing [its] impact is the extent to which those who have to take the decisions on the allocation of the nation's resources come

---

[12] *C.E.A.: Annual Report for 1968–69*, p. 5.

to accept its point of view'.[13] On this criterion, neither the Campaign nor the Council had a major influence. For both were created in the middle of a period of unprecedented growth in educational expenditure that began in the mid-1950s, and which continued at least until 1968. In each year after 1955, an ever increasing percentage of G.N.P. was spent on educational provision. But this trend did not markedly increase for the presence of either the Campaign or the Council, though conceivably it might have fallen for their absence.

As the table in Chapter 4 on the distribution of Government social expenditure since 1955 shows, 1963 marked the *end* of the period in which Government social expenditure had been moving in favour of education to the detriment of health and public housing.[14] The effect of the Campaign and Council here should have been to accentuate that trend, but in fact the distribution of social expenditure stabilised in 1964, and even moved slightly against education between 1963 and 1966. Before the Campaign, the N.E.D.C.'s *The Growth of the United Kingdom Economy to 1966* gave educational expenditure exactly the same growth rate as did *The National Plan* which came two years after the Campaign; and between these two documents, Government social priorities moved slightly against education in spite of the Campaign and the Council. The N.E.D.C., for example, gave education a growth rate of 5.7%, whilst allowing house building to rise 'at less than the rise in the gross national product of 4%'.[15] Not so *The National Plan*: it had public housing expanding by 33% in the five-year period, half a per cent *more* than education. Expenditure on roads and social security payments was equally to rise more rapidly than that on education under *The National Plan*.

At best, all that can be said is that the Campaign and the Council helped to prevent an even greater move away from education to health and public housing. This seems a fair assessment of the impact of the 1963 Campaign For Education. As its report said, 'the Government of the day has declared that it aims to make education its first priority...[and] this was not the state of affairs...when

---

[13] *The 1963 Campaign For Education: a report on its origins, work and achievements*, p. 4.
[14] Supra, p. 38.
[15] N.E.D.C. *The Growth of the United Kingdom Economy to 1966* (London, H.M.S.O. 1963), p. 45.

we decided...that a Campaign For Education was required'.¹⁶ But it is hard to see that the Council for Educational Advance had any impact at all on the political standing of education as an area of Government expenditure. It is worth considering why the impact of the two should possibly have been different.

THE CAMPAIGN AND THE COUNCIL COMPARED

The Vice-President of the 1963 Campaign For Education talked of the need for an 'educational crusade', a clear statement of a 'systematic, orderly, balanced programme of realistic objectives' and the creation of 'popular enthusiasm' for such a programme.¹⁷ The 1963 Campaign, and not the later Council, came nearest to providing education with a crusade of this kind. The support for the Campaign was wider, its local activity more sustained, and its strategy different from that of the Council that followed it; and on all of these dimensions it was better able to meet the initial purpose of its creation – 'to win public support and secure public action for general advance in education.'

As the Campaign organisers recognised, 'the most significant thing about [it was] that it unite[d] a large number of different organisations in pursuit of common aims'.¹⁸ Because of this, the Campaign could do what the teachers' associations alone could not, namely appeal to the political parties as the spokesman for a movement that united the educational world, and included many pressure groups beyond it. Yet the width of support for the alliance dwindled after 1963, and the Council lost a large part of its non-educational support, as Table 4 shows.

More important, the degree of involvement by the remaining associations was far less in the Council than in the Campaign. Officials of the smaller associations interviewed were unanimous in stressing both their involvement in the Campaign and their lack of interest in the Council, which had become, one said, far more a 'talking shop' than an educational crusade. The Council's organisers recognised from the outset that activity would be at a lower level than in 1963, but even they did not anticipate the paucity of local

---

¹⁶ *The 1963 Campaign For Education: a report*, op. cit. p. 4.
¹⁷ Dr L. White quoted in *Education*, 8 November 1963, pp. 885–6.
¹⁸ *1963 Campaign For Education: A Guide to Campaign Activity*, p. 11.

activity. Many of the already hard-pressed officials of the local associations involved in 1963 undertook activity then on the understanding that it was a once-and-for-all involvement; and successive Annual Reports of the Council for Educational Advance repeatedly note and regret the dearth of local activity.

Table 4. *The support for the Campaign and the Council*

	Campaign For Education	C.E.A. (Feb. 1965)	C.E.A. (mid-1969)
Educational bodies			
Teachers' associations	20	19	16
Local auth. assocs	1(3)‡	1(2)	1
Church bodies	7(2)	5(1)	6
Others*	23(1)	20(5)	17(1)
Total	51(6)	45(8)	40(1)
Trade unions†	29	19	14
Civic groups	5	5(1)	2
Industry	0(2)	0(2)	0
Others	1(1)	2	1§
Total	86(9)	71(11)	57(1)

* Including unions of educational workers.
† And professional bodies not in the education sector.
‡ The bracket indicates those associations with 'observer' status.
§ The Communist Party.

Yet it was primarily at local level that the 1963 Campaign aimed to create and to tap a 'groundswell of public opinion' in favour of educational advance, by the force of its publicity and by the involvement of parents locally in the work and problems of the schools. Denied this local support, the Council for Educational Advance had nothing to deliver to Governments but the co-ordinated views of its member associations at national level, who were anyway normally quite capable of taking their views to Government unaided by the Council. The Council could less validly say, as the Campaign had said, that substantial groups within the electorate at large supported its demands for educational advance. They may have, but the Council, denied local support, was in no position to know. Yet it was this popular support that appears to have given the Campaign whatever impact it had in the run-up to the 1964 General Election.

Reflecting and underpinning this difference in popular support for the Campaign and the Council was a difference in strategy that explains much of the difference in their respective impacts. The prime focus of the Campaign For Education was the political parties; that of the Council for Educational Advance became increasingly the D.E.S. itself. Yet the D.E.S. needed no convincing of the need for educational advance. The need was rather to persuade the Cabinet, of which the Department's political hand was only a middle-ranking member.[19] To achieve this, the 1963 Campaign tried to create a 'public opinion for educational advance' which it could then deliver to the Government through its impact on the electoral promises of the political parties. This was why its broad base of support and its many active local outlets were crucial, as a mechanism for generating a public opinion of this kind.[20]

Yet the Council for Educational Advance abandoned a strategy of preoccupation with the political parties after the 1964 General Election; and only revived the practice for that of 1966. Locally it lacked the organisation to even pressure election candidates in a sustained way; and in 1966, of 1,400 candidates approached, only 264 replied.[21] Instead, the Council took on two extra functions: of co-ordinating the policy of its member associations; and of 'policing' electoral promises. Then, submerged in the technical debates with the D.E.S. that these two functions produced, it lost sight of the initial goal of the 1963 Campaign, namely the creation of public opinion as an electoral pressure for educational advance.

For it was only for this latter task that the wide base of support for the Council was appropriate. Only if it could, like the Campaign before it, deliver a 'public opinion for educational advance' to the Government through the political parties, could it also safely spend

[19] As the C.E.A.'s Annual Report for 1965–6 recognised, the Council's deputations 'ought probably to have gone to see the Treasury, since the obstacles to what the Council was seeking appeared to reside there rather than at the D.E.S.' (*C.E.A. Annual Report*, 1965–6, p. 5).
[20] Obviously this strategy is particularly relevant before General Elections, but only a *sustained* 'public opinion for educational advance' could hope to protect education expenditure from 'cuts' between elections too. And the run-up to a General Election is often quite long, so the strategy need not be used only once every five years.
[21] *C.E.A.: Annual Report 1966–7*, p. 1.

time on 'policing' promises made. (In any case, its separate member associations could do this just as well.) But as co-ordination and policing become all, the Council could not mobilise the width of its alliance in support of its activity; and the alliance became moribund.

The impotence of this strategy of the C.E.A. – its preoccupation with co-ordination and policing without first generating a public opinion for educational advance – was clearest in 1968. By then, the Council controlled no coherent public opinion to stop the Labour Government placing the heaviest of its expenditure cuts on education. All that it could do was mobilise the bureaucracies of the teachers' associations and of the national educational bodies. It emerged as what it had become: a source of national press releases and conference resolutions that spoke for no-one but the representatives of the national associations affiliated to it, and co-ordinated the opinions of no-one but themselves.

The 1968 cuts might well have inspired the teachers' associations to revive a body to 'crusade' for education; and indeed the 1970 N.U.T. conference called upon the executive 'to campaign more intensively for a much larger share of the national resources for education'.[22] But by then, the larger associations had turned to an alternative kind of alliance to influence the distribution of public sector expenditure and the formation of national economic policy. They had turned to an alliance with organised labour.

[22] *The Teacher*, 10 April 1970, p. 3.

8
The Alliance with Organised Labour

Traditionally, the teachers' associations have been very reluctant to form permanent alliances with other sections of organised labour, and particularly with those organisations recruiting and representing manual workers. Yet Government policy in the 1960s, especially the 'pay pause' of 1961 and the growth of national planning and incomes policy that followed, threw into sharp relief the significance of national economic policy for the associations' influence within the education sector itself, and underlined their isolation both from other employee-organisations, and from the consultative processes at this level of decision-making. As a result, the teachers' associations in the 1960s sought channels of access to Government decision-making on national economic policy that were consistent with their position of political non-alignment.

They initially shunned affiliation to the T.U.C. because of its close ties to the Labour Party. Instead, the N.U.T., Joint Four and A.T.T.I. created the non-partisan Conference of Professional and Public Service Organisations, C.O.P.P.S.O., only for this to be destroyed by, ironically, a Conservative Government's preference for consultation with the T.U.C. alone. So that the larger associations have now affiliated to the Congress in spite of their previous reservations. In doing so, they have experienced the same range of arguments and debate that characterised the move into the T.U.C. of white-collar unions in the 1960s, and have indicated the major factors enabling the T.U.C. to recruit the majority of English white-collar unions by 1970.[1] Amongst these factors was the failure of C.O.P.P.S.O., which if it had succeeded would have constituted a teacher-dominated white-collar equivalent to the T.U.C., and which, in its failure, has been forgotten and little documented.

[1] For a parallel argument, see D. Volker, 'NALGO's affiliation to the T.U.C.', *British Journal of Industrial Relations*, vol. 4, March 1966, pp. 59–76.

THE CONFERENCE OF PROFESSIONAL AND PUBLIC SERVICE ORGANISATIONS

The formation of the Conference

When Selwyn Lloyd announced his 'pay pause' in July 1961, and with it rejected the Burnham settlement then pending, the N.U.T. formed two alliances. The first, an emergency committee of the main teachers' associations, did not survive the settlement of the immediate Burnham crisis. But the second, an alliance of white-collar associations, lasted longer, and became C.O.P.P.S.O., the Conference of Professional and Public Service Organisations.

The width of this alliance was determined by the nature of the 'pay pause'. For from the outset, the Government announced that it would impose the policy on its own employees, as an example to the private sector; so creating amongst organisations of public sector employees a common interest and sense of urgency. That the alliance was formed by the teachers' associations reflects a further feature of the 'pay pause', that it affected the Burnham Committee first.

The Conference first met in August 1961. Of the teachers' associations, the N.U.T. attended, with the A.T.T.I., the Joint Four and the Association of Teachers in Colleges and Departments of Education. Nine other white-collar organisations sent representatives,[2] and six sent observers.[3] At its peak in the spring of 1962, C.O.P.P.S.O. could speak for over 700,000 public sector and white-collar employees.

At this first meeting, Sir Ronald Gould stressed that 'they were not in any sense trying to set up a 'white-collar T.U.C.' or a new organisation in opposition to that body'.[4] Rather, this was to be an *ad hoc* organisation set up for a specific purpose ('to do a job and

---

[2] N.A.L.G.O., the Institute of Professional Civil Servants, the Association of Officers of Executive Councils and Pricing Committees, the British Gas Staff Association, the Confederation of Health Service Employees, the L.C.C. Staff Association, the Metropolitan Water Board Staff Association, and the Association of Scientific Workers.

[3] The Central Council of Bank Staff Associations, N.U.B.E., the British Dental Association, the B.M.A., the Engineers' Guild, and the Royal College of Nursing.

[4] *The Schoolmaster*, 1 September 1961, p. 346. Sir Ronald confirmed this in a private interview, 10 December 1969.

die', the *T.E.S.* reported him).⁵ Yet in spite of this, it is clear that the Union envisaged a more permanent role for the Conference, that of a teacher-dominated spokesman for 'professional workers', and a highly teacher-sensitive channel of access to decision-making on national economic policy. As such, it was a clear alternative to the T.U.C. and to its white-collar affiliate, the National Federation of Professional Workers. As Sir Ronald told the Conference, 'if any [consultative] body were to be established on which employers and employees were to be represented, it was of paramount importance that white-collar workers should have a voice on it'. For without a body such as C.O.P.P.S.O. 'the spoils would go to those who were industrially strong, and professional workers do not enjoy this sort of industrial strength'.⁶

The other organisations apparently shared the Union's definition of the role of the Conference. Even the Head Mistresses' Association welcomed the Conference as a means of bringing the views of professional workers to the notice of Government.⁷ Of the teachers' associations that attended, only the Headmasters' Association was cautious; its Executive Report records that its 'representatives urged moderation in the wording of a resolution, and finally co-operated in the interests of future relations with the N.U.T. over Burnham negotiations'.⁸ When these negotiations were over, the Headmasters withdrew.

In March 1962, the remaining associations agreed to establish formal machinery with limited and clearly defined functions. The Conference took the title of 'C.O.P.P.S.O.'; and agreed that major policy should be determined only by a full meeting of all the associations. A liaison committee was established to meet more frequently; and the Union continued to provide the Conference's secretariat and its first President. N.A.L.G.O. later provided its second.

---

⁵ *Times Educational Supplement*, 1 September 1961, p. 230.
⁶ *The Schoolmaster*, 1 September 1961, p. 346.
⁷ In its *Executive Report 1960–61*, the Association welcomed the Conference as a means of ensuring that 'professional, as well as industrial interests should have a share in the planning of future economic policy'.
⁸ *Review* of the H.M.A., December 1961, p. 119.

The activities of the Conference

Throughout its three and a half year existence, the Conference remained publicly critical of both the implementation and machinery of the Conservative's incomes policy. In August 1961, its first public statement expressed 'its strongest opposition' to the 'pay pause', and to its impact on the public sector, as being 'unjust, unreasonable and seriously damaging to good staff relations'.[9] In December it repeated its criticism, that the pay pause 'has not been and cannot be uniformly applied', and 'consequently...should be withdrawn, and full negotiation and arbitration procedures restored forthwith'.[10]

The Conference later criticised the Government's 'guiding light' incomes policy, as making no attempt to relate salary increases to the social value of the work performed, or to the needs of society for certain types of worker. It deplored the Government's treatment of the nurses' pay claim, as part of a more general criticism of the recent handling of the claims of public sector and professional employees. These, the Conference felt, provided 'additional evidence that the Government's "incomes policy" [could not] be justly applied, and was merely inflicting further hardships on the groups whose salaries and wages already [fell] substantially below those of comparable groups in the private sector'.[11]

Nor was C.O.P.P.S.O. any more impressed by the machinery of incomes policy. It was highly critical of the National Incomes Commission, which it saw as a threat to existing negotiating machinery, and a continuation of the policy of discrimination against public sector employees. Though keen to participate in the National Economic Development Council, the Conference announced its 'lack of confidence' in any Council from which it was excluded.

This question of N.E.D.C. representation dominated the Conference from its first meeting with Selwyn Lloyd, in September 1961. The Chancellor told the Conference deputation of his intention to create the Council, as a forum through which the Government could consult employers and workers on future economic policy – the latter through the T.U.C. The Conference immediately requested representation; but all that Lloyd would concede at this first meet-

[9] *The Schoolmaster*, 1 September 1961, p. 346.
[10] *N.U.T. Annual Report*, 1962, p. 66.
[11] *The Schoolmaster*, 1 June 1962, p. 1383.

ing was 'that the point was important, and [he would] consider it, but would give no promise'.[12]

When the N.E.D.C.'s membership was announced in February 1962, C.O.P.P.S.O. was given no seat; and Sir Ronald Gould wrote to the Chancellor, suggesting direct representation of the Conference on the Development Council. This, Lloyd rejected. The Council, he replied to Sir Ronald, 'is not a "representative body" and must in any event be limited in numbers'.[13] All that he was prepared to offer was a possibility of representation to the N.E.D.C. by individual organisations, or by C.O.P.P.S.O., on particular issues.

This did not satisfy either the Conference, or the N.U.T. Without C.O.P.P.S.O.'s representation on the N.E.D.C., the Union felt that groups lacking industrial power would have little chance of parity of treatment and in particular, income policy would continue to discriminate against public sector employees. Nor was the Conference impressed by Selwyn Lloyd's reasons for its exclusion. Why, if the N.E.D.C. was not a representative body, did the Government go to such lengths to secure T.U.C. co-operation? Sir Ronald wrote again to the Chancellor, asking him to reconsider.[14]

> While we fully appreciate the need for the T.U.C.'s representation on the Council, it is the opinion of our Conference that the views of the members of its constituent organisations...are not represented on the N.E.D.C. We can have no confidence...that as at present constituted it will concern itself with the specific needs of the people we represent....In our view the case for giving our Conference representation...is strengthened by the fact that the groups it represents are not, primarily, engaged in work with a precisely measurable end product. If the N.E.D.C. discusses 'the proper relationship between increases in income and increases in production' without giving special consideration to the role of those not engaged in productive industry, and without the benefit of first-hand advice from those directly concerned, we feel it will only help to perpetuate the sense of injustice which so many professional and public service employees feel at the present time.

[12] A. Spoor, *White Collar Union: Sixty Years of N.A.L.G.O.* (London, Heinemann, 1967), p. 295.
[13] *The Schoolmaster*, 16 March 1962, p. 650.
[14] *The Times Educational Supplement*, 6 April 1962, p. 687.

But Selwyn Lloyd remained unconvinced, and a further request in June 1962 was no more successful. A new Chancellor brought no change of Government policy. Though the Conference again pressed for recognition for consultative purposes, Reginald Maudling refused it membership of the N.E.D.C. as Lloyd had done before.

The collapse of the Conference

C.O.P.P.S.O.'s last meeting was held in February 1965, only to agree that the Secretary (and therefore the N.U.T.) could reconvene the Conference if a change in the national economic situation and the position of public servants made this necessary. But as the constituent bodies began to withdraw (N.A.L.G.O. and the Association of Broadcasting Staffs joined the T.U.C.) even this vestige of organisation was abandoned.

There are two major reasons for the Conference's failure. The changing nature of incomes policy after the 'pay pause' sapped the common interests, and sense of urgency, that had united its constituent organisations in 1961.[15] Incomes policy between 1962 and 1966 was less rigorously applied; and (crucial for the maintenance of the Conference's rationale) did not discriminate overtly against public sector employees. The alliance might have found a new rationale, as the permanent spokesman for 'professional' and 'white-collar' interests, if it had won a place on the emerging consultative machinery for national planning. But it did not; and with no clear common interest, and a growing sense of impotence, its constituent associations withdrew.

C.O.P.P.S.O. had been created to give its white-collar organisations a form of non-partisan[16] access to Government decision-making on national economic policy in general, and incomes policy in particular. If it had succeeded, the N.U.T. would have created a channel of access to such decision-making that would have been highly receptive to the views of the teachers' associations. With its failure, no other channel of access existed that could be so receptive.

By 1965, as before 1961, only the T.U.C. and its affiliate, the N.F.P.W., remained as this route to Government decision-making

---

[15] See C. M. Phillipson, 'A Study of the Attitudes towards and Participation in Trade Union activities of selected groups of non-manual workers' (M.A. thesis University of Nottingham, 1964), p. 149.
[16] 'Non-partisan' in the sense of clearly not linked to any political party.

on national economic policy that the Union had sought to create in C.O.P.P.S.O. But now, the Conservative's clear preference for the T.U.C. had reduced its partisan appearance,[17] and with Labour in power, there was even less hope that a separate federation of white-collar workers would be granted consultative status. The debate turned to the question of T.U.C. affiliation.

AFFILIATION TO THE TRADES UNION CONGRESS

The opponents of affiliation to the T.U.C. in the 1960s argued that it would involve an alliance with the Labour Party, was in any case unprofessional, and would have unfortunate repercussions on both the level of membership and the search for professional unity. It would overburden association officials, and cost large sums of money, without providing any noticeable increase in the influence of those associations. Against these, the advocates of affiliation denied that membership of the T.U.C. was incompatible with the associations' policy of political non-alignment. They pointed to the increasing number of white-collar organisations already affiliated and to the general sympathy between the T.U.C.'s educational goals and those of the teachers. They doubted if affiliation would cause many members to leave, or impair the autonomy of the separate associations. They argued repeatedly that it was no longer sufficient to concentrate pressure on the D.E.S. alone. Only the T.U.C. would provide teachers with access to Government decision-making on national economic policy. The power of this last argument has already carried the three largest associations into the T.U.C.

The arguments against T.U.C. affiliation

That affiliation involved an alliance with the Labour Party has been

[17] The advocates of affiliation made much of the Conservative Party's reaction to N.A.L.G.O.'s affiliation to the T.U.C. in 1964. Joseph Godber, Shadow Minister of Labour (the Conservatives were by then out of office) gave the move Conservative support. He wrote, 'N.A.L.G.O.'s recent affiliation...is of great significance for the Trade Union movement...Conservative policy is to encourage and support democratic trade unionism...We certainly welcome any move which will produce greater cohesion and co-ordination within the Trade Union Movement' (*N.U.T. Annual Report*, 1966, p. 55).

a predominant fear of the opponents of T.U.C. membership. In 1920, when the N.U.T. executive first considered affiliation, its likely impact on the Union's policy of non-alignment, and on its system of sponsoring M.P.s, was a major cause of the decision to reject alliance with the trade unions.[18] This was still a serious impediment in the 1960s. An executive memorandum in 1966, while recognising that 'there is no doubt that the Union could maintain its non-party political status if it affiliated', insisted that 'there are T.U.C./Labour Party links' which would make it difficult to persuade many Union members of this.[19] The memorandum gave this as the first of three reasons for rejecting affiliation; and similar arguments occurred frequently in the parallel debates on affiliation in the N.A.S. and A.T.T.I.

In addition, opponents of affiliation argued that it would be 'unprofessional' to ally teachers' associations with the T.U.C. At one extreme, virulent anti-unionism appeared frequently in the debate on affiliation. More moderate analyses merely stressed that teachers' associations were not 'trade unions' but 'professional associations', sharing neither interests nor methods with unions of manual workers. A *Schoolmaster* editorial in 1962 defended C.O.P.P.S.O. in these terms, as an organisation whose 'aims, aspirations and methods were totally different' from those of the T.U.C.

> The Union's claim to public notice has always been quite different from that of those bodies of workers which draw their strength from the Congress. Our strength, like that of the doctors [a much favoured reference group in arguments of this type] lies not in our productivity, which cannot be measured, but in our professional expertise. The economic considerations on which the T.U.C. members argue their pay demands are not the same as ours.[20]

This lack of congruence in the goals and methods of the teachers' associations and those of the T.U.C. and its member unions was particularly stressed by opponents of affiliation within the N.A.S.

[18] D. Thompson, *Professional Solidarity amongst the Teachers of England* (New York, Columbia University Press, 1927), p. 216.
[19] 'Affiliation to the Trades Union Congress; a statement and proposals prepared by the Executive and approved by the Annual Conference, 1966', in *N.U.T. Annual Report 1966*, pp. 52–7 (from now *N.U.T. Memo. 1966*). These quotations, p. 55 and p. 57.
[20] *The Schoolmaster*, 14 September 1962, p. 16.

The T.U.C. had long championed 'equal pay' for women, against which the Association fought from its foundation. Union members made the same point, in recalling the N.U.T.'s hostility to the imposition of a closed shop in Durham in 1952, and its traditional reluctance to take strike action. They compared both with what they took to be the normal trade union methods of compulsory membership and the withdrawal of labour.

These views were sufficiently widespread and articulated to create a fear that affiliation to the T.U.C. would drive many teachers from the associations. The N.U.T. executive in 1966 made this the second 'weightiest consideration' leading them to oppose affiliation.[21] 'The maiden ladies in Rutlandshire', as one young teacher called them, were keeping the Union out of the T.U.C. by the threat of their defection. This was an argument used by the secretary of the A.M.A. to explain Joint Four reluctance to affiliate; namely that any such move into the T.U.C. 'would cause serious splits in each of the Joint Four's constituent associations'.[22]

The N.U.T. executive in 1966 feared that affiliation 'would entail an abandonment of [the Union's] policy of professional unity based on negotiations'.[23] Even in recommending affiliation to the 1968 conference, a later executive repeated this fear: that 'it is likely that professional unity would be harder to achieve if the N.U.T. decided to seek affiliation...[it] would probably make negotiations more difficult if not almost impossible for some considerable time'.[24]

N.A.S. opponents of affiliation warned of the A.T.T.I.'s experience in the T.U.C. The rise in A.T.T.I. fees, one claimed, was a direct result of 'the increased financial contribution exacted by their masters at Congress House'.[25] This cost, the critics said, would be incurred with no return to the teachers' associations. The Secretary of the A.M.A. told the Headmasters' Association in conference, 'I can see no reason for taking a decision which would so weaken us when for the life of me I can see no compensatory benefits from joining'.[26]

[21] *N.U.T. Memo. 1966*, op. cit. p. 56.
[22] *The Teacher*, 10 April 1970, p. 4.
[23] *N.U.T. Memo. 1966*, op. cit. p. 56.
[24] 'Affiliation to the Trades Union Congress; a statement and proposals prepared by the Executive for submission to the Annual Conference 1968', p. 6 (from now, *N.U.T. Memo. 1968*).
[25] *The Times Educational Supplement* (letter to), 26 April 1968, p. 1392.
[26] Ibid, 10 April 1970, p. 10.

The arguments for T.U.C. affiliation

The executives of the A.T.T.I., N.A.S. and N.U.T. have, between them, issued seven documents of affiliation since 1963.[27] All agreed that affiliation was compatible with the policy of political non-alignment. The N.A.S. was satisfied that political impartiality 'would not be jeopardised';[28] the A.T.T.I., that their 'policy of non-alignment...will not be changed if the Association affiliates'.[29] 'There is no doubt', the Union executive reported in 1968, that the N.U.T. 'could maintain its non-party political status if it affiliated'.[30] They had not denied this even when rejecting affiliation in 1966; all that they had doubted then was that many Union members could be persuaded that this was so.

With N.A.L.G.O.'s affiliation in 1964, the N.U.T. became the largest professional group outside the T.U.C., and N.A.L.G.O.'s experience was a much quoted example of the entry of white-collar unions into the Congress in the 1960s. The N.U.T.'s 1968 memorandum listed, without comment, 22 affiliated public service unions, of which N.A.L.G.O. was the largest. The N.A.S. insisted that 'important white-collar unions...have joined the T.U.C. during the last few years, and have helped to modify the "cloth cap" image'.[31] And the arguments of professional exclusiveness that had supported C.O.P.P.S.O. were cast aside by the second Union memorandum. The T.U.C., it said, no longer discriminates against white-collar workers, and if it did, 'the argument can fairly be made that...it is better to affiliate and make sure by fair representation that the case of the white-collar worker is heard and appreciated'.[32] Advocates of affiliation stressed the general sympathy existing between the goals of trade unions and those of the teachers' associa-

---

[27] The N.U.T. memos of 1966, 1968 and 1970; the N.A.S. Memo, of 1968; and three documents from the A.T.T.I., one in 1963 and two in 1968. All advocated affiliation except the N.U.T. Memo. of 1966, which opposed affiliation, and the A.T.T.I. document of 1963, which made no recommendation.
[28] 'N.A.S.: T.U.C. Affiliation – a report submitted by Executive to Conference 1968' (from now on *N.A.S. Memo 1968*), p. 1.
[29] The *Technical Journal*, December 1966, p. 3.
[30] *N.U.T. Memo. 1968*, op. cit. p. 5.
[31] *N.A.S. Memo. 1968*, op. cit. p. 1.
[32] *N.U.T. Memo. 1968*, op. cit. p. 4.

tions, and the strengthening of these ties that affiliation would bring.

By 1968, and in the light of the experience of N.A.L.G.O. and the A.T.T.I., the N.U.T. executive were less certain than they had been in 1966 that affiliation would produce large membership defections. Their second memorandum was less pessimistic than the first, and left the matter open. Each executive stressed that affiliation would involve no loss of autonomy on the part of the teachers' associations. 'Affiliated unions', the N.A.S. said, 'retain complete autonomy; neither the Congress nor the General Council can over-ride decisions of an affiliated union.'[33] The N.U.T. agreed: 'the Union, if affiliated, would not...be committed to policies which it did not accept or which had been rejected by its own Annual Conference'.[34]

Yet such arguments merely sought to remove the obstacles to T.U.C. affiliation created by the opponents of this link with organised labour. As such, they provided no motive for affiliation; nor do they explain the renewed interest in the T.U.C. after thirty years without discussion. Affiliation became an issue in the 1960s not because of any specific sympathy between trade union and teacher goals, or because it could be achieved without loss of political nonalignment. These arguments merely facilitated a move prompted by the realisation that, with the failure of C.O.P.P.S.O., the T.U.C. had become the only channel through which the teachers' associations might exert influence on the formulation of national economic policy. A search for influence carried the larger associations into the T.U.C. in the second half of the 1960s.

The isolation of non-affiliated associations from decision-making on national economic policy was the major recurrent theme in the debate on affiliation. The first N.U.T. memorandum was unique in discounting its importance. The second memorandum formulated the problem precisely:

> There is general agreement that the Union should endeavour to exercise and intensify its influence on relevant national policies. There is, however, a divergence of opinion on whether this can be more effectively achieved in the coming years by the Union continuing its policy of a self-contained professional organisation

[33] *N.A.S. Memo. 1968*, op. cit. p. 2.
[34] *N.U.T. Memo. 1968*, op. cit. p. 5.

co-operating on an *ad hoc* basis on educational problems, or by the Union, whilst continuing to co-operate on an *ad hoc* basis with other bodies, to affiliate to the Trades Union Congress to increase and widen its sphere of influence.[35]

The choice for the associations was between restricting their activities to pressure on the D.E.S., within constraints set by Government expenditure priorities and by national economic policy established elsewhere, or supplementing this pressure by joining the T.U.C., as the only means of access to decision-making outside the education sector. With the failure of C.O.P.P.S.O. and the Government's creation of machinery through which to involve the T.U.C. in regular consultation in economic policy, the events of the 1960s repeatedly underlined the unaffiliated associations' isolation from decision-making both on public sector expenditure priorities and on national economic policy. On the N.E.D.C., in the drawing up of the Declaration of Intent, on the National Plan, on the formulation of incomes policy after the 'freeze' of July 1966, and in the cuts in Government expenditure after devaluation, the T.U.C. was consulted and the teachers' associations were not.

The executives' memoranda bear testimony to the impact of this. The N.U.T. in 1968: if 'the Union is to have any real and effective voice in the establishment of educational priorities in the general economic planning then it must be closely involved with the work of the T.U.C.'.[36] The N.A.S. also:

> No doubt the strongest argument for affiliating...in present day circumstances is that [the T.U.C.] is recognised as a kind of Estate of the Realm, representing the interests of organised workers in almost every field. If an organisation wishes to have some say in shaping the views of the Congress on the wide issues of economic, social and educational policy, it can only do so by joining.[37]

For the Technical Teachers too, the main motive taking the Association into the T.U.C. was its isolation from decision-making on national economic policy. In its 'memorandum of guidance' to

[35] *N.U.T. Memo. 1968*, op. cit. p. 3.
[36] Ibid, p. 3.
[37] *N.A.S. Memo. 1968*, op. cit. p. 4.

the 1966 special conference that preceded affiliation, the executive wrote:

> Economic planning machinery is being evolved by which the Trade Unions and organised industry act in an advisory capacity in the determination of national economic policy. Membership of the T.U.C. would enable the Association to have a more direct influence on this machinery.
>
> This planning apparatus, which involves expenditure on educational buildings and equipment as well as salaries, has far reaching implications for the education service in general, and further education in particular. The Association should, therefore, seek direct influence on the determination of priorities.[38]

THE AFFILIATION OF THE A.T.T.I.

The A.T.T.I. affiliated to the T.U.C. on 1 January 1967, amidst the kind of internal dissension that the N.A.S. and N.U.T. were later to experience. Its executive first circulated a document on affiliation to members of its Council in January 1964. Of all the memoranda that the executives of the three largest associations issued in the 1960s, this first one alone contained no recommendation either for or against affiliation.

It simply described the organisation, work and aims of the Congress, and its relationship both to the Labour Party and to its member unions; it listed the non-manual unions in the Congress; gave the financial cost of affiliation and described in detail the T.U.C.'s Education Committee. But in tone it was cautiously favourable to affiliation. It contained no list of disadvantages but suggested at least two possible benefits of formal links between the teachers and the T.U.C. It suggested that the Congress's Education Committee 'could be strengthened considerably through teacher representation',[39] and noted the possible implications of the T.U.C.'s involvement in, and C.O.P.P.S.O.'s exclusion from, the National Economic Development Council.

There was insufficient support within the Association for T.U.C.

[38] 'A.T.T.I.: Memorandum on affiliation to the Trades Union Congress (1966)', pp. 3-4.
[39] 'A.T.T.I.: Memorandum on affiliation to the Trades Union Congress (1963)', in the Agenda for the January 1964 Council, p. 21.

affiliation to be debated at conference in 1964, or to allow it more than the last ten minutes of debate in 1965. But by 1966, a call for immediate affiliation was high on the conference agenda, with an executive amendment proposing a referendum of the membership. The conference rejected a referendum, voting 115 to 56 for immediate affiliation. Only the calling of a special conference by opponents of the move prevented the A.T.T.I. from joining the T.U.C. in the summer of 1966.

This special conference was held in October. Before it, the executive issued a 'memorandum of guidance' by reprinting their 1963 document with an additional section recommending affiliation. Mr Tom Driver spoke for the executive, arguing strongly that the Association affiliate. 'It was clear to everybody', he said,

> ...that in the present day major decisions of policy affecting our members were being taken by large and influential bodies on which at the moment we had no influence. The incomes policy was being decided between the T.U.C., the Government, and the C.B.I. and we had to operate within that and get the best we could. It was the Executive's view that we should play at any rate a small part if no more in the decision-making. Secondly, the Executive considered that we could have greater influence on educational thinking if we were in a position to influence the T.U.C.[40]

The special conference agreed; and the A.T.T.I., which had joined the National Federation of Professional Workers in the autumn, joined the T.U.C. on 1 January 1967.

THE AFFILIATION OF THE N.A.S.

The N.A.S. was the first of the teachers' associations to vote for affiliation to the T.U.C. It held a referendum in 1943; but the poll was low, and the majority, though in favour, was small, and consequently no action was taken.[41] The Association was also the first to join the N.F.P.W. It did so in 1966, on the intiative of its General

[40] 'A.T.T.I.: Special Conference on T.U.C. affiliation – 15 October 1966, (Report of)', p. 1.
[41] G. Latta, 'The N.A.S. – a historical analysis' (unpub. M.Sc. thesis, University of Warwick, 1969).

Secretary and without consulting its membership, in order to 'come into closer contact with Civil Service and other public service unions who share some of the problems facing teachers'.[42]

The N.A.S. conference in 1962 called for a consideration of T.U.C. affiliation, but there was insufficient agreement on the executive to enable it to make any recommendation. The issue was not raised again within the Association until 1967 when the executive, again largely on the initiative of its General Secretary, circulated a memorandum in favour of affiliation.

This memorandum followed the N.U.T. executive's change of policy in favour of affiliation, and was in part a reaction to it. The N.A.S. feared that if the Union affiliated, it would be effectively excluded from the T.U.C.; and 'the N.A.S. must not become isolated. We would be at a serious disadvantage in the 1970s if we allow hostile interests to make it virtually impossible for us to join the T.U.C. because they had secured an entrenched position.'[43] Later A.T.T.I. opposition from within the T.U.C. to the entry of the N.A.S. substantiated these fears without preventing its affiliation.

This fear of exclusion was more acute because the executive recognised that outside the Congress, the Association would continue to be isolated from decision-making on national economic policy.

> The T.U.C. is actively concerned with economic and educational questions which closely affect our interests; the government seeks its advice on national insurance, pensions, negotiating procedures and many other topics affecting the general interests of employees. Unless we stake our claim to have our interests considered, those who shape T.U.C. policy will feel no obligation to take them into account.[44]

The memorandum was considered by conference in 1968, and a call for a referendum successfully opposed. Affiliation was supported by a card vote; and after waiting for the result of the N.U.T. referendum in the autumn, the N.A.S. went in alone to the T.U.C. in November 1968.

[42] *N.A.S. Memo. 1968*, op. cit. p. 4.
[43] Ibid, p. 1.
[44] Ibid. p. 1.

THE AFFILIATION OF THE N.U.T.

The call for N.U.T. affiliation to the T.U.C. was first raised in the 1890s, but was decisively rejected by conference in 1895. It reappeared in 1917 and in 1920, and on both occasions was rejected by the Union executive. From then on, the question of affiliation received less and less attention. It was debated at conference in 1939, and not again until 1965.

The advocates of T.U.C. affiliation claimed for their motion a new significance in the 1960s; that it offered a means of access to the emerging machinery of economic planning. But the lesson was initially lost on the executive, even though it was not consulted in negotiations leading to the 'Declaration of Intent' that heralded Labour's incomes policy. For the Union instead asked the Secretary of State for Education and Science to discuss the incomes policy with them, and were impressed at the speed with which their request was granted. So that initially under Labour, the Government's preference for the T.U.C., so evident under the Conservatives, appeared muted; and the question of access to decision-making on national economic policy was not taken as the prime issue by the executive as it formulated the memorandum for which the 1965 conference had called.

This memorandum specifically stated that *The National Plan*, and the T.U.C.'s 'early warning system' within the incomes policy, were 'not relevant to the broader questions of affiliation to the T.U.C.'.[45] Rather, the executive was preoccupied with the effect of affiliation on the Union's policy of non-alignment, its search for organisational unity, and on the probability of membership defection. On all three counts, it rejected affiliation.

Yet as Sir Ronald Gould made clear in his critique of the National Plan,[46] Union leaders were aware that they lacked access to decision-making on national economic policy. But they still looked for means of access other than the T.U.C. to policy-making at this level. If the Government 'is really in earnest about consultation and consent', Sir Ronald Gould said, 'it should establish consultative machinery for bodies...who for various reasons, are not members

[45] *N.U.T. Memo. 1966*, op. cit. p. 54.
[46] Supra, pp. 42–43.

of the T.U.C.'.⁴⁷ The Union even declined to affiliate to the N.F.P.W. Only when the Union's appeal for direct consultation with the Department of Economic Affairs was rejected (by the Secretary of State, the Union-sponsored Michael Stewart) did the executive reconsider T.U.C. membership.

For when the Union asked Michael Stewart to receive a deputation, to discuss the place of Burnham settlements in the incomes policy after 'the period of severe restraint', they were referred to the Secretary of State for Education and Science.⁴⁸ The supporters of affiliation made much of this reply. 'Mr Stewart has been compelled to say', one executive member claimed, 'that he could not even meet his own members because Government policy was to consult only the Confederation of British Industries and the Trades Union Congress.'⁴⁹

In the second memorandum on affiliation, drawn up in 1967, the executive realised the dilemma that Michael Stewart had presented: 'whether in these circumstances [the Union] can play a more effective part by continuing normal consultative relationships with the Department of Education and Science and the Local Authority Organisations, or augmenting them through affiliation to the T.U.C.'.⁵⁰ After discussions with N.A.L.G.O., the A.T.T.I., and with Mr Victor Feather of the T.U.C., the executive recommended affiliation if supported by a referendum of the membership.

But the N.U.T. did not affiliate immediately, since the referendum, in October 1968, failed to provide the necessary majority. In a low poll (only 30% of the Union voted), the proposal to affiliate was rejected by a ratio of 4:3. But the executive was committed by the 1969 conference to campaigning within the Union for 'the understanding and acceptance' of affiliation;⁵¹ and its Finance and General Purposes Committee decided early in 1970 to urge affiliation at the 1970 conference. There, the executive proposal for immediate affiliation, without a referendum, was carried by a clear majority;

---

⁴⁷ *National Planning and the Education Service* (London, College of Preceptors, 1966), p. 16.
⁴⁸ This was a peculiarity of the D.E.A. under Michael Stewart. When the Department of Employment and Productivity took over responsibility for incomes policy later, it regularly saw individual unions.
⁴⁹ Max Morris, quoted in *The Teacher*, 24 February 1967, p. 4.
⁵⁰ *N.U.T. Memo. 1968*, op. cit. pp. 3-4.
⁵¹ *The Times Educational Supplement*, 4 April 1969, p. 1093.

and the Union joined the N.A.S. and A.T.T.I. in the T.U.C. on 1 May 1970.

THE FUTURE OF THE ALLIANCE

It remains to be seen how important this new alliance with organised labour is for the teachers' associations in the 1970s, and indeed whether any or all of the associations leave the T.U.C. in the unlikely event of that body dividing on its attitude to the Industrial Relations Act of 1971. The negligible impact of T.U.C. lobbying on the level of unemployment and the pattern of economic growth in the early 1970s suggests that the change in actual influence resulting to the teachers' associations from affiliation will probably be limited; but it is precisely the absence of sustained and substantial economic growth that constantly underwrites, for the associations and their members, the importance of national economic policy for their own bargaining position within the education sector.

The associations are not likely to abandon lightly the only formal channel of access that they currently possess to the formulation of national economic policy. The use they (and other unionists) make of that channel will turn on the calibre of their leadership, and more crucially, on the character of the political and industrial awareness of the rank and file membership of the associations. One factor shaping that awareness will be their general understanding of the potentialities and limitations of the strategies and tactics adopted by their associations in the 1960s. Here at least, perhaps, studies of this kind have a limited but useful contribution to make.

9
The Determinants of Interest Group Behaviour

The argument hitherto has stayed close to the detailed experience of teacher politics in England and Wales. The pattern of stability and change in the strategies and tactics adopted by the teachers' associations in their search for influence has been explained as a product of the associations' continuing experience of success, frustration and failure – as that pattern of success and failure has changed the associations' understanding of the power relationships that they face and of the strategies and tactics open to them. This indeed is how the associations' leaders appear to have seen the process. The changes in behaviour that they have instituted have been – more often than not – *ad hoc* responses to unanticipated situations, the full implicacations of which became clear to them only in restrospect. In this sense, the changing behaviour of the associations grew out of their own experience of teacher politics in the 1960s.

But the nature of the choice of strategies and tactics that the associations faced was not random; nor, as Chapter 4 made clear, were the actual choices that they made unconnected. There is an underlying logic in the pattern of behaviour adopted by organised teachers in the 1960s – the logic of a systematic attempt to gain access to, and influence over, the changing structure of decision-making that the associations faced, and to whose rulings their teacher-members were subject. Put schematically, when the Education Department enjoyed the autonomy to take the vast majority of the decisions which the teachers' associations required, the associations naturally focused the bulk of their activity on that Department. To the degree that the D.E.S. still enjoys that autonomy, that focus remains. But as the constraints which surrounded the D.E.S. became more potent and more visible in the 1960s – constraints which flowed from the Department's relationship with other spending Departments, the Cabinet and the Treasury – so the teachers' associations came slowly to recognise the need both to strengthen their hand before a weakened Department and to gain access to decision-making points outside the education sector itself.

Couched in these terms, the argument has relevance only for the teachers' associations of England and Wales. Yet the power relationships that they faced, and the impact of those relationships on the behaviour that they adopted, were not unique to organised teachers. The experience of the teachers' associations was similar to that of many interest groups facing Central Government in the 1960s. Arguments about the determinants of the behaviour of teachers' associations, therefore, might have a relevance for the behaviour of a wide range of organised groups attempting to influence the decision-making processes of Government. For this reason, it seems useful to attempt to bridge the ideographic and the nomothetic in the study of interest group politics, by couching an argument about the determinants of the behaviour of organised teachers in terms that could be more generally applicable. This could both illuminate the experience of the teachers' associations and facilitate a wider test of the argument being put forward.

THE BEHAVIOUR TO BE EXPLAINED

Interest group behaviour, as was explained in the Preface, can be taken to encompass the strategies and tactics adopted in the search for influence, where strategy involves the choice of a power centre to be lobbied, and tactics are understood to be the means adopted to lobby the power-centre chosen. On this understanding, there are four major characteristics of the behaviour of organised teachers which have to be explained.

The first is a marked continuity in the *range* of strategies and tactics adopted over time.[1] The strategies used by the teachers' associations in 1960 (and those on which in the main they continued to rely thereafter) were first adopted before 1900: namely attempts to influence the Department of Education and the local authorities, contacts with M.P.s and the occasional mobilisation of public opinion. Each association still sent memoranda and deputations to

---

[1] 'A continuity in range' means simply that all the strategies and tactics used in period X were *known* to the associations in period (X–1). It implies nothing about the importance attached to any particular strategy and tactic in any particular period – a continuity in range, for example, could be (and for the teachers' associations, was) fully compatible with marked shifts of emphasis away from some behaviour in the range over time.

the Department of Education and Science, wrote letters and sent petitions and local deputations to individual M.P.s, and briefed journalists – tactics known to the teachers' associations in the last quarter of the nineteenth century.

But continuity in the range of strategies and tactics used is not the only feature of their behaviour. Over the century, there has been a shift of emphasis within that traditional range: a shift in strategy, away from the local authorities and Parliament and towards the Education Department; and a change in tactics, away from irregular and formal contacts with the Education Department to a regular and more informal relationship.

The third feature of the behaviour of organised teachers that requires explanation is their unprecedented *extension* of this traditional range of strategies and tactics in the 1960s. As we have seen, the teachers' associations supplemented their traditional forms of behaviour by the new or revived tactics of organisational unity, professional self-government and national scale militancy; and by new strategies – attempts to influence centres of government decision-making beyond the system of educational administration by alliances with both educationally-minded interest groups and organisations of labour.

Finally, the behaviour of organised teachers is characterised – at one and the same time – by marked similarities *and* important differences in the strategies and tactics adopted by the various associations. The forms of behaviour established in the last quarter of the nineteenth century were common to all associations, though each differed slightly in the range of behaviour it traditionally used. Parliamentary action always played a greater role for some (noticeably the N.U.T.) than for others; and informal contacts were established earlier by the Joint Four than by the N.A.S.[2] In the 1960s, the associations differed markedly in their attitudes to, and participation in, the new strategies and tactics adopted. They differed in their attitude to a single teachers' organisation, and in the use of militancy. They differed in their commitment to the Council for Educational Advance, and in their attitude to C.O.P.P.S.O.; and only three of the eight associations affiliated to the T.U.C. These differences between the associations have also to be explained.

[2] And not just because the N.A.S. was formed later. Even in the 1950s, the N.A.S. had a more formal relationship with the Ministry than had either the Joint Four or the N.U.T.

THE ELEMENTS OF THE ANSWER

Hitherto students of interest group politics have explained the strategies and tactics adopted by interest groups in one of two ways. More normally they have asserted or assumed that group behaviour is a pragmatic response to certain dimensions of the *environment* faced by the interest group; and in particular to the impact of three dimensions of that environment – the structure of administration faced, the policy of government, and the political culture shared by interest group and government alike. Almond, Beer, Rose, Castles, Wootton, Macridis and Clark all explain patterns of interest group behaviour in these terms;[3] and in so doing, follow the arguments specified most clearly by Eckstein, that 'basically, it is always the interplay of governmental structure, activities, and attitudes which determines the form of pressure group politics'.[4]

Alternatively, the strategies and tactics adopted by organised groups have been explained in terms of the *organisational* characteristics of the group itself. Far from asserting, with Eckstein, a total sensitivity of behaviour to environmental pressures, the alternative argument stressed the mediation of such environmental factors through character-dimensions of the organisation concerned. This second explanation of organisational behaviour has been most systematically developed in studies of the activity of white-collar trade unions, of which the teachers' associations, of course, are a major example. So Allen, Routh, Strauss, Kleingartner, Lockwood, Blackburn and Prandy have all argued for differences of degree or of kind between white-collar and manual union behaviour, behav-

---

[3] G. Almond, 'A comparative study of interest groups and the political process', *American Political Science Review*, vol. 52(1), March 1958, p. 278; S. Beer, 'Pressure groups and parties in Britain', *American Political Science Review*, vol. 50(1), March 1956, pp. 11–16; R. Rose, *Politics in England* (London, Faber, 1965), pp. 130–2; F. G. Castles, *Pressure Groups and Political Culture* (London, Routledge and Kegan Paul, 1967), *passim*; G. Wootton, *Interest Groups* (New Jersey, Prentice-Hall, 1970), p. 46; R. Macridis, 'Interest groups in comparative analysis', *Journal of Politics*, vol. 23, 1961, p. 41; J. M. Clark *Teachers and Politics in France* (New York, Syracuse University Press, 1967), pp. 165–84.

[4] H. Eckstein, *Pressure Group Politics* (London, Allen and Unwin, 1960), p. 17).

ioural differences which they explain as the product of the different social position of their respective memberships.[5] Industrial militancy and alliances with organisations of manual workers are here taken to be either impossible or difficult for white-collar trade unions precisely because, as Allen said, white-collar workers such as teachers cannot easily dispense with 'the middle class values...which have led them in the past to denigrate crude industrial action'.[6]

Neither of these explanations of interest group behaviour seems adequate to accommodate the complex patterns of strategy and tactics adopted by organised teachers. The precise nature of their inadequacy should become clear as the chapter progresses, and will be considered in detail at its end. For the moment it is worth noting that neither of them adequately locate all the 'environmental' and 'organisational' dimensions that shape group behaviour; nor do they stress sufficiently the interaction of these factors in the determination of group strategies and tactics. For the behaviour of the teachers' associations of England and Wales can be most profitably explained by reference to the interaction of, on the one hand, not three but *four* aspects of a largely shared environment, and on the other, of at least three aspects of organisational character.

The strategies and tactics adopted by organised teachers were primarily a response to (1) the changing *structure* and (2) the changing *policy* of Government that they faced. The changing structure and policy of Government – which constituted the changing context

---

[5] V. L. Allen, 'Trade unions in contemporary capitalism', *Socialist Register 1964* (New York, Monthly Review Press, 1964), pp. 172–3; G. Routh, 'United Kingdom', in A. Sturmthal (ed.), *White Collar Trade Unions* (London, University of Illinois Press, 1966), p. 165; G. Strauss, 'White collar unions are different', *Harvard Business Review*, vol. 32, September–October 1954, p. 73; A. Kleingartner, 'The organisation of white collar unions', *British Journal of Industrial Relations*, vol. 6(1), March 1968, p. 83; D. Lockwood, *The Blackcoated Worker* (London, Allen and Unwin, 1958), p. 198; R. M. Blackburn and K. Prandy, 'White collar unionisation, a conceptual framework', *British Journal of Sociology*, vol. 16(2), July 1965, pp. 111–22.

[6] V. L. Allen, op. cit. pp. 172–3. It may be noted that Eckstein indicated that such group characteristics might 'deflect' groups from the optimal pattern of strategy and tactics suggested by his three environmental dimensions. But such organisational variables were explicitly secondary in his analysis which made 'the power structure of government a more decisive desiderata, than the power base of the group' (Eckstein, op. cit. pp. 20–1).

of bargaining for organised teachers in the 1960s[7] – brought the associations face-to-face with the relationships of power within which they sought influence. Its impact on their behaviour was mediated through two subsidiary sets of factors. For the precise strategies and tactics that they adopted were affected by other features of the environment faced by organised teachers; by (3) the *accessibility* of this changing structure and policy of Government to the associations, and by (4) the *pattern of other interest group activity* that surrounded it. Teacher behaviour was affected too by characteristics of the associations themselves, not least by the nature of the (1) *goals*, (2) *memberships*, and (3) *leadership* that each association brought to bear on the changing context of their bargaining.

Because the behaviour of the teachers' associations was affected by so many different factors, no single factor can be said to have dictated any single pattern of behaviour. But nonetheless it is possible to isolate in principle the contribution of each factor in turn; and this we will do, before returning to the question of the overall determination of interest group behaviour.

THE IMPACT OF 'ENVIRONMENT' ON BEHAVIOUR

Sructure

The prime strategy of the teachers' associations – their preoccupation with the Department of Education – was conditioned by two trends in the distribution of effective power within the structure of British Government. The first, at national level, shifted power laterally from Parliament to Department; the second, within the system of educational administration, shifted power vertically from individual local authorities to the national Departments of Government. At national level, the creation of a system of disciplined political parties moved power from Parliament to the Cabinet, where the growth of Government activity shifted it to the administrative Departments (in this case, to the Department of Education and Science). Within the system of educational administration, the continuing requirement for standardised educational provision, and the growing cost of educational programmes, strengthened the position

---

[7] Supra, Chapter 4, *passim*.

of the national administrative Department and local authority associations, this time against locally elected and locally appointed officials alike.

Neither trend in structure was total, and this also was reflected in the strategy of the teachers' associations. Nationally, Parliament still provided a secondary arena for pressure on the detail of educational legislation; and the D.E.S. was not autonomous as a unit of decision-making within the structure of Government. The control of the Cabinet over expenditure priorities, and the Treasury's *de facto* control of the growth rate of public expenditure, drew the teachers' association towards these points of decision-making in the 1960s. Nor were the local authorities mere adjuncts of the Central Government. They retained decision-making rights over a wide range of issues; and the teachers' associations were organised locally to bring pressure to bear on this level of decision-making, and pressured the national associations of local authorities to this same end.

But the majority of issues on which the teachers' associations sought influence fell within the discretion of the Department of Education, and this single fact is the major explanation of the degree to which the associations shared a predominant and unchanging strategy. It was also a prime environmental influence on tactics. For, as Stewart said, 'the techniques of pressure direct on the ministries are the techniques of consultation'.[8]

Policy

Neither the strategy nor the tactics of the teachers' associations were immune from the impact of Government policy; and to grant primacy to 'structure' alone would be to forget that only 'policy' gave the structure of Government its significance for the behaviour of organised teachers. Structure and policy overlapped in a number of ways in shaping strategy and tactics.

In the first instance, teachers were led to organise associations through which to pressure Government only when the State began to develop educational policy in the 1830s. Obviously the preoccupation of the teachers' associations with the D.E.S. and its predecessors was, and is, a reflection of their interest in the type of policy for which the Department of Education was primarily responsible; and

[8] J. D. Stewart, *British Pressure Groups* (Oxford, at the Clarendon Press, 1958), p. 29.

the growing closeness of the relationship between the associations and the Department was as much a product of the Department's own need for advice, acquiescence and approval as the scale of its activity increased, as the product of any pressure from the teachers' associations themselves. The growth of policy drew the associations to the Department, and took the Department towards the interest groups that surrounded it.

In the 1960s, the points of change in the strategy and tactics of the teachers' associations largely reflected the changing nature of this relationship between Government structure and policy. The policy of educational expansion, requiring an ever increasing share of G.N.P. for educational provision, led the associations to focus on the political parties, as a means of strengthening the Cabinet's commitment to educational advance. Equally, departures in policy made relevant new points in Government structure, and occasioned new strategies and tactics. So the tentative attempts at national planning and the development of incomes policy, transferred issues previously left to the discretion of the D.E.S. to decision-making processes centred on other Departments, and inspired the changing strategy of the teachers' associations. C.O.P.P.S.O. and T.U.C. affiliation were tactical alliances resulting from the modification of strategy that followed these policy initiatives.

Government policy also affected the strategy and tactics of the associations independently of its relationship with the structure of Government, through what can be termed 'a feedback of failure'. On the level of strategy, the failure of the associations to influence policy made at one point of Government structure led them, on occasions, to turn to other parts of that structure in a search for influence. So Sir Edward Boyle's decision in 1963 to reject a Burnham settlement led the N.U.T. to organise a major *Parliamentary* campaign in an attempt to reverse that policy, after direct approaches to the Ministry had failed. Nor were tactics immune from this failure to influence policy. In 1967 and 1969, the associations' failure to negotiate a salary settlement in excess of the prices and incomes policy norm led the N.U.T. (in 1967) and the N.U.T., the N.A.S. and the A.M.A. (in 1969–70) to take militant action in support of their salary demands.[9]

[9] Wider Government policy also played a part here, in permitting prices to rise, and overall rates of earnings to increase, more than the incomes policy norm applied to the teachers.

The accessibility of Government[10]

The accessibility of the Department of Education to the pressure of the teachers' associations strengthened the cumulative impact of the structure and policy of Government that they faced, by drawing them towards the Department and into a private consultative relationship. Each of the officials interviewed confirmed this accessibility of Departmental personnel and Ministers to the associations; and some commented on the changing nature of this access over time. In the early days of each association, access, even when available, was on formal terms. 'You wrote a letter and waited months', one Assistant Secretary said. By the 1960s, Departmental officials could be contacted by telephone, seen privately, met in working parties or on advisory committees, and Ministers were normally available at very short notice. The key to the growing informality of the associations' relationship with the Department lay here, in the increased willingness of its officials to consult them privately, regularly and at all stages of the policy-making process.

But Government structure was not open to all the associations all the time. Nor was it open to them at all points; and their behaviour reflected this lack of access too. Before 1961, the N.A.S. was denied membership of the advisory committees surrounding the Department, and lacked the informal relationship with Departmental personnel that the N.U.T. and the Joint Four enjoyed. Without the right of informal and regular access, the cumulative effect of structure and policy could not be carried to its logical conclusion. Rather access became itself an N.A.S. goal and all parts of the Government structure were approached in order to win it from the Department. The strategy and tactics of the Association before 1961 reflected the lack of this access as much as the high degree of uniformity in the behaviour of the other associations reflected its possession.

Even in the 1960s all the teachers' associations lacked access individually to centres of Government decision-making other than the D.E.S.; and this too affected the form of their new behaviour in the decade. They had no direct access to the Cabinet, which determined the priorities of social expenditure crucial to the growth rate of educational provision. Nor were they granted access to either the

---

[10] On the relationship of this dimension of environment to what Beer and Eckstein call 'culture', see later.

Department of Economic Affairs or to the Treasury, which saw only the peak organisations on either side of industry, and the finance institutions.[11] The Council for Educational Advance, C.O.P.P.S.O. and T.U.C. affiliation were all tactical alliances adopted to win collective access to points of Government structure closed off to the associations separately.

In any event, access was given only on certain terms, and the associations' tactics responded to what Finer called 'the code', and Nettl, 'the predictable and well-mannered Whitehall methods'.[12] Deputations, advisory committees, working parties, memoranda, and personal contacts were all channels of access allowed to the teachers' associations by the Department of Education, which the associations used in their search for influence. Equally M.P.s were open to access only on certain terms. These could be formal – such as the rules of Parliamentary privilege – or informal, such as the unpopularity of repeated mass lobbies.[13] The associations' relationship with Parliament reflected both.

The pattern of other interest group activity

Aspects of Government were not the only dimensions of environment faced by the teachers' associations. Both the existence of other interest groups and the pattern of their relationships with Government, were autonomous factors influencing the associations' choice of strategies and tactics.

At one extreme, the existence of other teachers' associations inspired competititve behaviour. N.A.S. militancy after 1961 may be partly explained in this way, as an attempt to draw off members from the N.U.T. Equally, the existence of other interest groups allowed a number of forms of coalition within the education sector:

---

[11] S. Brittan, *Steering the Economy* (London, Secker and Warburg, 1969), p. 25.
[12] S. E. Finer, *Anonymous Empire* (London, Pall Mall Press, 2nd ed., 1966), p. 33; and P. Nettl, 'Consensus or elite domination; the case of business', *Political Studies*, vol. 13(1), February 1965, p. 33.
[13] So that, e.g., when considering whether to organise a *second* mass lobby against Sir Edward Boyle's Remuneration of Teachers Act in 1963, the N.U.T. took the advice of one of its sponsored M.P.s that 'it would be irritating...M.P.s would refuse to go out to it a second time...There can be a far more effective lobby if we have a smaller number of people' (*The Teacher*, 26 April 1963, p. 7).

between the teachers' associations themselves on a common issue, such as a Teachers' General Council; with local authority associations, on the change in the grant structure; or in as wide an alliance of educationally-minded interest groups as could be found, to campaign for educational advance. In addition, the associations found that to win access to other centres of decision-making required alliances across the boundaries of the education sector; and the willingness of certain of the associations to participate in these broader alliances enabled their strategy to take in points of Government policy-making that they had hitherto ignored.

ORGANISATIONAL CHARACTERISTICS AND BEHAVIOUR

Though structure, policy, accessibility and the pattern of other interest group activity suggested optimal strategies and tactics, they did not themselves determine behaviour. For the significance of each for the behaviour of organised teachers varied with the goals, membership characteristics and leadership of each association in turn.

Organisational goals

In principle three types of goals can be distinguished for the teachers' associations – their most general goal, or *function*; and more specific goals, *policy goals* which relate to the detail of legislation or administrative regulations; and *institutional goals*, generated by the need of each association to maintain itself.[14]

Clearly the associations shared their most general level of goals. Their common concern to influence decision-making processes of Government that affect teachers produced a common definition of the distribution of effective power. All came to attach greater importance to national pressure than to local activity; and at national level all came to direct their attention primarily towards the Department of Education and only secondarily towards Parliament. The *institutional* goals of the associations divided them; and on the detail of educational legislation or regulations, each stressed the interests of particular groups within the teaching force, which overlapped and coincided on certain issues and conflicted on others.

[14] On this distinction see A. S. Tannenbaum 'Unions' in J. G. Marsh (ed.), *Handbook of Organisations* (Rand McNally, Chicago, 1965), p. 718.

These differences in goals were reflected in the associations' differing responses to the new forms of behaviour of the 1960s. The search for organisational unity was primarily motivated by the N.U.T.'s desire to reduce the impact of sectional organisation on the effectiveness of its pressure; and was rejected by the other associations because of their commitment to organisational autonomy. The pattern of N.A.S. militancy, as has already been noted, was at least partly a product of the Association's attempt to recruit N.U.T. members. The shared commitment of the associations to educational advance led them to support the 1963 Campaign For Education and the later Council for Educational Advance; and their differing degrees of concern with salary policy (and the differing content of their salary policy) was reflected in the different responses of the associations to C.O.P.P.S.O. and the T.U.C.[15]

Characteristics of the membership

The characteristics of the membership of the teachers' associations were predominantly common. With the exception of the tiny proportion of Joint Four members who taught in private schools, all were serving teachers employed by L.E.A.s in England and Wales. That is, they taught in schools subject to the legislation and administrative regulations administered by the D.E.S. within terms and conditions of service which were centrally negotiated and nationally applied. These common membership characteristics reinforced strategy suggested by the environmental dimensions of structure, policy and accessibility, in that they pulled the associations towards the D.E.S.

Yet within this common framework, the associations' memberships differed in their size, in their occupational position, qualifications and training, and in the volatility and substance of their attitudes to industrial militancy. Each of these differences affected the patterns of behaviour realistically open to the leadership of each of the associations. *Size*, for example, made Parliamentary lobbying a

---

[15] Since such alliances were adopted to influence, amongst other things, incomes policy they were of central interest to associations like the N.U.T. for which salary questions were of crucial importance, and less so to associations like the Headmistresses' Association, for which salary issues were secondary in importance to other 'educational' issues.

more attractive proposition to the N.U.T. than to the smaller associations; just as the *occupational prestige* (and associated social position) of the members of the Headmasters' Associations 'opened' the Department of Education to their informal pressure long before the larger N.U.T. established such a relationship. And the changing *attitude* of large sections of the teaching profession to the use of militant tactics opened a new range of behaviour to the leaders of the larger associations by the end of the 1960s. The N.U.T., after all, abandoned militancy in 1961 when its membership failed to give overwhelming support to strike action. Yet by 1969, the executive of the Union were reluctantly led to reverse their salary policy, and adopt militant tactics, in the face of a spontaneous outburst of teacher militancy that affected even the Joint Four.

Leadership

It should be no surprise that leadership is singled out as one determinant of the strategy and tactics adopted by the teachers' associations. For with the exception of the periods of mass militancy, the behaviour considered here has involved *only* leadership behaviour, in associations in which the existence of formally democratic processes of internal government still leaves (as in most unions) immense freedom of action to executive committees and to full-time national officers. This is not to discount totally the impact of annual delegate conferences on the policy and behaviour of the associations. There were occasions – around T.U.C. affiliation for example – on which such conferences played a crucial role in determining strategies and tactics adopted. But such examples are rare in the internal politics of the teachers' associations. The annual conferences had enough difficulty establishing some degree of control over the detailed policy pursued, and settlements made, by their national leaderships; and invariably focused on this. The question of the strategies and tactics to be adopted in the pursuit of any policy normally went undiscussed, and the decision passed – if only by default – to the full-time officers and executive committees charged with the pursuit of policy between annual delegate conferences.[16]

At certain points in the 1960s, leadership played a crucial role in

[16] Even those critical of the quality of Union leadership have granted it a major impact of behaviour; see, e.g. R. A. Manzer, *Teachers and Politics* (Manchester, Manchester University Press, 1970), pp. 150–1.

changing association strategies and tactics. The formation of the 1963 Campaign For Education, and later the Council for Educational Advance, was largely the result of one man's initiative – that of Fred Jarvis, then head of the Publicity and Public Relations Department of the N.U.T. The Conference of Professional and Public Service Organisations was formed on the initiative of the Union's executive. The N.A.S. joined the N.F.P.W. and later the T.U.C. largely as a result of its General Secretary's commitment to affiliation. The N.U.T. voted on affiliation only when its executive, by a change of personnel and a realignment of attitude among certain of its members, had come to support the idea.

THE BEHAVIOUR OF THE TEACHERS' ASSOCIATIONS EXPLAINED

The four features of the behaviour of the teachers' associations isolated earlier can now be explained in these terms. The associations' traditional concern with the Department of Education, with Parliament and with public opinion was a product of the cumulative impact of Government *structure*, *policy* and *accessibility* on associations with a high degree of similarity of *function*, of *membership* and of *leadership*. Their traditional use of the tactics of consultation, of links with M.P.s and with the press, followed from this traditional strategy, as a response to the optimal techniques of pressure suggested by the points of Government structure approached.

The changing emphasis in both strategies and tactics within this continuity of range (away from Parliament and the local authorities to the D.E.S.; and before the Department, from formal and irregular to informal and regular means of contact) were the product of changes in Government *policy* and *structure* (which moved decision-making on issues central to the teachers' associations from local to national level, and from the Legislature to the Executive); and of changes in the *accessibility* of the Department to the activity of the associations themselves.

The new strategies of the 1960s (attempts to bring pressure to bear on the Cabinet through the political parties, and on the Treasury, D.E.A. and D.E.P.) were a response to developments in Government *policy* that impinged visibly on the teachers' associations, and so increased the relevance of these other centres of decision-making. The new tactic of militancy was a response to the impact on the

Burnham Committee of the emerging *policy* on prices and incomes that was made elsewhere in the structure of Government. The new alliance forged with organised labour reflected both the lower degree of teacher *accessibility* to these alternative centres of power; and the existence around these power centres of an already established *pattern of group activity* which offered the associations an indirect route of influence.

Finally, the difference and similarities in the behaviour of the associations can be explained in these terms. That all the associations shared a similar traditional strategy reflected the degree to which related *goals*, similar *memberships*, and *leaderships* working in close proximity, led the associations to give a similar definition to the strategic requirements of a *largely shared environment*. The difference of emphasis within the traditional forms of behaviour reflected both the degree to which Government structure was less open to some associations than to others, and the degree of difference in the *membership characteristics* of each association. The greater difference in the associations' involvement in the new behaviour in the 1960s reflected the different definition given to the significance of the *policy* changes of the decade by each of the associations: itself a product of different emphases in their *goals*, different *attitudes* amongst their members, and the different nature of their *leaderships*.

That is, the dimensions of 'environment' that the teachers' associations faced suggested certain optimal strategies and tactics for each. To the degree that this 'environment' was common to all the associations, it evoked a common behavioural response from the organisational characteristics that they shared. But to the degree that dimensions of their environment differed for each association and to the degree that organisational characteristics differed between them, so the relationship between 'environment' and 'organisation' conditioned a different pattern of behaviour from each. As the 'environment' that the associations faced changed, and as organisational characteristics of each modified, so the associations adopted new forms of behaviour.

THE ANALYSIS OF INTEREST GROUP BEHAVIOUR

It should now be clear that neither the 'environmental' nor the 'organisational' explanations of interest group behaviour are adequate alone. Organisational characteristics offer no unambiguous guide to the strategies and tactics adopted, precisely because each new form of interest group behaviour is primarily a response to a particular environment of bargaining, a response not determined but only conditioned by the organisational features of the associations themselves. In consequence, it is unsafe to deduce from any single pattern of behaviour any membership characteristic peculiar to the association under view, without first controlling for changes in the environment within which that pattern of behaviour is played out. The teachers' experience underwrites this clearly. T.U.C. affiliation, for example, tells us little (if anything) about the changing consciousness of class amongst unionised teachers, but much about the changing structure, policy and accessibility of Government, faced by the teachers' associations in the 1960s. Even teacher militancy, which is certainly a more reliable indicator of membership attitudes, cannot fully be explained without reference to the pattern of Government policy against which militant action was taken.[17]

Equally, there is no simple relationship between 'environment' and behaviour. It is true that, in line with Eckstein's argument, the strategies and tactics of the teachers' associations again demonstrate the impact of Government structure and Government policy on behaviour. But they also demonstrate the role of a dimension of 'environment' hitherto given little if any importance, namely the pattern of other interest group activity;[18] and where Eckstein sees the impact of society-wide attitudes, or 'culture', on the behaviour of pressure groups, the experience of the teachers' associations suggests that the dimension has been mis-specified, and could more appropriately be called 'the accessibility of Government'.

For in the case of the teachers' associations, attitudes influenced behaviour only when they were linked to centres of power. Attitudes to interest groups, for example, shaped strategies and tactics because, and only to the degree that, they were held by the personnel in the centres of Government decision-making (that is, by Departmental officials or M.P.s) that the associations approached. The accessibility

---

[17] For a full consideration of the relationship between membership characteristics and aspects of union character see G. S. Bain, R. D. Coates and V. Ellis, *Trade Unions and Social Stratification* (forthcoming).

[18] This dimension has been noted by J. D. Stewart, op. cit. p. 43; and G. Wootton, *The Politics of Influence* (London, Routledge and Kegan Paul, 1963), p. 7.

of Government was therefore *both* a set of attitudes and an actual degree of access granted by different units in the structure of Government. These attitudes might indeed dictate the degree of access given – to this extent the term 'culture' might be relevant – but it was the degree of access itself, rather than the attitudes alone, that shaped strategy and tactics.

Nor were the attitudes to interest groups necessarily as broad and indiscriminate as the use of the term 'culture' implied. There could indeed be society-wide values, common to the environment of all interest groups, that suggested certain patterns of behaviour. But for the teachers' associations, the openness of Government was not simply a generalised value, or a universally equal degree of access. It was also a highly specific set of attitudes (and resulting degrees of access) that were unevenly distributed between units of Government structure, between associations, and over time. That is, some parts of Government were more open to the teachers' associations than were others. Some associations enjoyed greater degrees of access than did others. A single teachers' association could enjoy greater access to one point in Government than to another; and the granting of access could be given or withdrawn. As such, 'the accessibility of Government' was a constraint on the behaviour of the teachers' associations, in that it suggested (as did the other dimensions of 'environment') certain optimal strategies and tactics.

More generally, the argument that interest group behaviour (including that of the teachers' associations) was a product of 'environmental factors' failed to make clear that behaviour was a product of 'environment' only as that 'environment' was conditioned by its impact on dimensions of 'organisation'. None of the new strategies and tactics adopted by the teachers' associations in the 1960s was a simple response to changes in the 'environment' faced. The adoption of militant tactics required a marked change in membership attitudes, and both the alliance for educational advance and that with organised labour were adopted only after leadership initiatives. Even organisational unity which, if Eckstein is correct, should have followed the growth of Central Government power,[19] was frustrated by organisational characteristics which a full analysis of behaviour must incorporate.

Such a full analysis of interest group behaviour necessarily involves

[19] Thus, 'Pressure groups tend somehow to resemble the organisations they seek to influence', H. Eckstein, op. cit. p. 21.

a detailed assessment of the complex interaction of dimensions of the environment faced by an interest group and characteristics of the organisation itself. The environment faced should be understood as a set of power relationships that condition the strategy and tactics of the organisation by setting limits on its effectiveness. Equally the dimensions of organisation singled out in the explanation of teacher behaviour suggest that a power dimension is operating within the organisation too, offering yet another set of constraints on the freedom of manoeuvre of elected and appointed officers alike. It was these sets of power relationships faced by the leaders of the teachers' associations that tightened markedly in the 1960s, to leave – on certain issues at least – a mobilised rank and file face-to-face with an intransigent Government. With Governments still trapped by low rates of economic growth and the competing demands of other public services, the scene appears set for successive confrontations with militant teachers in the 1970s.

Bibliography

Studies of this kind are highly dependent on sources not generally available: on interviews with leading officials of the teachers' associations, and on the associations' journals and private memoranda. Equally, the study drew at times on unpublished theses and government publications. Where such sources support the text, they have been footnoted; and there seems little point listing them separately at the end. So the bibliography that follows is restricted to published secondary material; and is divided – somewhat arbitrarily no doubt – into literature primarily concerned with educational government and literature of more general relevance for the wider study of interest group politics.

1. LITERATURE ON EDUCATIONAL POLITICS

Alexander, W. P. *Education in England* (London, Newnes Educational Publishing Company, 2nd ed., 1964).

Armytage, W. H. C. *Four Hundred Years of English Education* (Cambridge University Press, 1964).

Baron, G. 'The teachers' registration movement', *British Journal of Educational Studies*, vol. 2(2), May 1954, pp. 133-45.

Brand, J. A. 'Ministerial control and local autonomy in education', *Political Quarterly*, vol. 36(2), 1965, pp. 154-63.

The Burnham Story (London, Councils and Education Press, 1963).

Clark, J. M. *Teachers and Politics in France* (New York, Syracuse University Press, 1967).

Coates, R. D. 'The teachers' associations and the restructuring of Burnham', *British Journal of Educational Studies*, June 1972, pp. 192-204.

Cole, S. *The Unionisation of Teachers* (New York, Praeger, 1969).

College of Preceptors, *Teachers Guide 1964-5* (London, the College of Preceptors, 1965).

Conway, F. 'An index of teachers' salaries', *Bulletin of the Oxford University Institute of Statistics*, vol. 15, numbers 6 and 7, June 1953, pp. 237-48.

'School teachers' salaries 1945-1959', *Manchester School of Economic and Social Studies*, vol. 30, May 1962, pp. 153-80.

Cruikshank, H. *Church and State in English Education* (London, Macmillan, 1963).

Curtis, S. J. *Education in Britain since 1900* (London, Andrew Dakers and Co. 1952).

Dent. H. C. *Growth in English Education 1946-1952* (London, Routledge and Kegan Paul, 1954).

The Educational System of England and Wales (London, University of London Press, 1966).
Gosden, P. H. J. H. *The Development of Educational Administration in England and Wales* (Oxford, Blackwell, 1966).
Gould, Sir Ronald. *National Planning and the Education Service* (London, College of Preceptors, 1966).
Gretton, J. 'Cloth cap teachers', *New Society*, 28 May 1970, pp. 909–11.
Kekewich, G. *The Education Department and After* (London, Constable, 1920).
Kogan, M. *The Politics of Education* (Harmondsworth, Penguin, 1971).
Lester Smith, W. O. *Government of Education* (Harmondsworth, Penguin, 1965).
Maclure, S. 'The Control of Education', History of Education Society, *Studies in the Government and Control of Education since 1860* (London, Methuen, 1970), pp. 1–12.
Manzer, R. A. *Teachers and Politics: the role of the National Union of Teachers in the making of national educational policy in England and Wales since 1944* (Manchester, Manchester University Press, 1970).
Margerison, C. J. and Elliott, C. K. 'A predictive study in teacher militancy', *British Journal of Industrial Relations*, vol. 8(3), November 1970, pp. 408–17.
Morris, N. 'England', in A. A. Blum (ed.), *Teachers' Unions and Associations: a Comparative Study* (London, University of Illinois Press, 1969).
Leggatt, T. 'Teaching as a profession', in J. A. Jackson (ed.), *Professions and Professionalisation* (Cambridge, Cambridge University Press, 1971).
Parkin, H. *Key Profession* (London, Routledge and Kegan Paul, 1969).
Price, P. 'The Teachers' strike', in K. Coates *et al.* (ed.), *Trade Union Register 1970* (London, The Merlin Press, 1970).
Roy, W. 'Membership participation in the N.U.T.', *British Journal of Industrial Relations*, vol. 2(2), 1964, pp. 189–208.
The Teachers' Union (London, The Schoolmaster Publishing Company, 1968).
Selby-Bigge, L. A. *The Board of Education* (London, Putman, 1927).
Taylor, W. *The Secondary Modern School* (London, Faber, 1963).
Thompson, D. *Professional Solidarity Among the Teachers of England* (New York, Columbia University Press, 1927).
Tropp, A. *The School Teachers* (London, Heinemann, 1957).
Vaizey, J. *The Costs of Education* (London, Allen and Unwin, 1958).
Teaching in a Modern Economy (London, College of Preceptors, 1963).
Education for Tomorrow (Harmondsworth, Penguin, 1962).
Vaizey, J. and Sheehan, J. *Resources for Education* (London, Allen and Unwin, 1968).
Webb, B. *English Teachers and their Professional Organisation* (a special supplement to *The New Statesman*, vol. 5, no. 129, 25 September 1915 and vol. 5, no. 130, 2 October 1915).

2. LITERATURE ON INTEREST GROUP BEHAVIOUR

Allen, V. L. 'Trade unions in contemporary capitalism', *Socialist Register 1964* (New York, Monthly Review Press, 1964). pp. 157–74.

Almond, G. 'A comparative study of interest groups and the political process', *American Political Science Review*, March 1958, vol. 52(1), pp. 270–82.

Annals, 'Unofficial Government; pressure groups and lobbies', *Annals* 319, September 1958.

Bain, G. S. *The Growth of White Collar Unionism* (Oxford, at the Clarendon Press, 1970).

Bain, G. S., Coates, R. D. and Ellis, V. *Social Stratification and Trade Unionism* (forthcoming 1973).

Beer, S. H. 'Pressure groups and parties in Britain', *American Political Science Review*, vol. 50(1), March 1956, pp. 1–23.

'The representation of interests in British Government', *American Political Science Review*, vol. 51(3), September 1957, pp. 613–50.

Modern British Politics (London, Faber, 1965).

Beer, S. H. and Ulam, A. B. *Patterns of Government* (New York, Random House, 2nd ed. 1962).

Blackburn, R. *Union Character and Social Class* (London, Batsford, 1967).

Blackburn, R. M. and Prandy K. 'White collar unionisation: a conceptual framework', *British Journal of Sociology*, July 1965, pp. 111–22.

Bray, J. *Decision in Government* (London, Gollancz, 1970).

Bridges, Lord. *The Treasury* (London, Allen and Unwin, 1964).

Brittan, S. *Steering the Economy: the Role of the Treasury* (London, Secker and Warburg, 1969).

Butt, R. *The Power of Parliament* (London, Constable, 2nd ed., 1969).

Castles, F. G. *Pressure Groups and Political Culture* (London, Routledge and Kegan Paul, 1967).

'Business and Government: a typology of pressure group activity', *Political Studies*, vol. 17(2), June 1969, pp. 160–77.

Caves, R. E. *et al. Britain's Economic Prospects* (London, Allen and Unwin, 1968).

Chester, D. N. *Central and Local Government* (London, Macmillan, 1951).

Chester, D. N. and Willson, F. M. G. *The Organisation of British Central Government, 1914–1964* (London, Allen and Unwin, 2nd ed., 1968).

Christoph, J. B. *Capital Punishment and British Politics* (London, Allen and Unwin, 1962).

Cyriax, G. and Oakeshott, R. *The Bargainers: a Survey of Modern Trade Unionism* (London, Faber, 1960).

Eckstein, H. *Pressure Group Politics* (London, Allen and Unwin, 1960).

Ehrmann, H. W. *Interest Groups on Four Continents* (Pittsburgh, University of Pittsburgh Press, 4th printing, 1967).
'The comparative study of interest groups.' Paper to the Congress of the I.P.S.A., Rome, September 1958 (Geneva, I.P.S.A., 1958).
Finer, S. E. *Anonymous Empire* (London, Paul Mall Press, 1st ed., 1958, 2nd ed., 1966).
'Great Britain', in Macridis and Ward (eds.), *Modern Political Systems: Europe* (New Jersey, Prentice Hall, 1968).
Griffith, J. A. G. *Central Departments and Local Authorities* (London, Allen and Unwin, 1966).
Harrison, M. *Trade Unions and the Labour Party since 1945* (London, Allen and Unwin, 1960).
Hindell, K. *Trade Union Membership* (London, Political and Economic Planning, 1962).
Key, V. O., Jr. *Politics, Parties and Pressure Groups* (New York, Thomas Y. Crowell Company, 2nd ed., 1947).
Kleingartner, A. 'The organisation of white collar unions', *British Journal of Industrial Relations*, vol. 6(1), March 1968, pp. 79-93.
LaPolombara, J. 'The utility and limitations of interest group theory in non-American field situations', *Journal of Politics*, vol. 22(1), February 1960, pp. 29-49.
Longley, L. 'Interest group interaction in a legislative system', *Journal of Politics*, vol. 29(3), August 1967, pp. 637-59.
Mackenzie, W. J. M. 'Pressure groups in British Government', *British Journal of Sociology*, vol. 6(2), June 1955, pp. 133-48.
Macridis, R. 'Interest groups in comparative analysis', *Journal of Politics*, vol. 23, 1961, pp. 25-45.
Millett, J. H. 'The role of an interest group leader in the House of Commons', *Western Political Quarterly*, vol. 9(4), 1956, pp. 915-26.
'British interest group tactics: a case study', *Political Science Quarterly*, vol. 72(1), March 1957, pp. 71-82.
Nettl, P. 'Consensus or elite domination; the case of business', *Political Studies*, vol. 13(1), February 1965, pp. 22-44.
Political and Economic Planning, *Advisory Committees in British Government* (London, P.E.P., 1960).
Political Quarterly, 'Symposium: Pressure Groups in Britain', *Political Quarterly*, vol. 29(1), January-March 1958.
Potter, A. 'British pressure groups', *Parliamentary Affairs*, vol. 9(4), Autumn 1956, pp. 418-26.
'The Equal Pay Campaign Committee: a case study of a pressure group', *Political Studies*, vol. 5(1), March 1957, pp. 49-64.
Organised Groups in British National Politics (London, Faber, 1961).
Report of the Select Committee on Delegated Legislation (London, H.M.S.O., 1953).
Rose, R. *Politics in England* (London, Faber, 1965).
Routh, G. 'United Kingdom', in A. Sturmthal (ed.), *White Collar Trade Unions* (London, University of Illinois Press, 1966).
Sartori, G. *Pressure Groups or Interest Groups*. Paper submitted to

Congress of the I.P.S.A., Rome, September 1958 (Geneva, I.P.S.A., 1958).

Self, P. and Storing H. *The State and the Farmer* (London, Allen and Unwin, 1962).

Spoor, A. *White Collar Union: Sixty Years of N.A.L.G.O.* (London, Heinemann, 1967).

Stewart, J. D. *British Pressure Groups: their role in relation to the House of Commons* (Oxford, at the Clarendon Press, 1958).

Strauss, G. 'White collar unions are different', *Harvard Business Review*, vol. 32 (September–October 1954), pp. 73–82.

Tannenbaum, A. S. 'Unions', in J. G. Marsh, *Handbook of Organisations* (Chicago, Rand McNally, 1965).

Truman, D. *The Governmental Process* (New York, Alfred A. Knopf, 2nd ed., 1953).

Vernon, R. V. and Mansergh, N. (ed.), *Advisory Bodies: a Study of their uses in relation to Central Government 1919–1939* (London, Allen and Unwin, 1940).

Volker, D. 'NALGO's affiliation to the T.U.C.', *British Journal of Industrial Relations*, vol. 4, March 1966, pp. 59–76.

Walkland, S. A. *The Legislative Process in Great Britain* (London, Allen and Unwin, 1968).

Wilson, H. H. *Pressure Group: the Campaign for Commercial Television* (London, Secker and Warburg, 1961).

Wiseman, H. V. *Politics in Everyday Life* (Oxford, Blackwell, 1966).

Wootton, G. *The Politics of Influence* (London, Routledge and Kegan Paul, 1963).

Interest-Groups (New Jersey, Prentice Hall, 1970).

Index

Advisory Committees 6, 10, 11
Assistant Masters Association (*see also* Joint Four)
  and Sir Edward Boyle 27
  and Campaign For Education 83–93 *passim*
  conferences of 23, 24
  executive of 25, 124–5
  formation 1, 2
  membership 3, 4
  and militancy 60, 61, 72, 74, 76, 80
  and organisational unity 2, 4–5, 47–52
  and professional self-government 52–7
  and pension scheme 21–6
  publicity 17–19
  relations with M.P.s 15, 16, 121
  and the T.U.C. 102
Association of Assistant Mistresses (*see also* Joint Four)
  and Campaign For Education 83–93 *passim*
  conferences of 23
  formation 1, 2
  membership 3
  and organisational unity 2, 4–5, 47–52
  and pension scheme 21–6
  and professional self-government 52–7
  and militancy 72, 74
Association of Broadcasting Staffs 95, 99
Association of Education Committees 5
Association of Head Mistresses (*see also* Joint Four)
  and Campaign For Education 83–93 *passim*
  conferences of 23
  and C.O.P.P.S.O. 96
  formation 1, 2
  membership 3
  and organisational unity 2, 4–5, 47–52
  and pension scheme 21–6
  and professional self-government 52–7
  and militancy 72
Association of Municipal Corporations 5, 7, 30
Association of Teachers in Colleges and Departments of Education 53, 95
Association of Teachers in Technical Institutions
  and Sir Edward Boyle 27
  and Campaign For Education 83–93 *passim*
  conferences of 23, 24–5, 26, 57, 107
  and C.O.P.P.S.O. 94, 95
  executive of 102, 106, 107, 124–125
  formation 2
  membership 3–4
  and militancy 72
  and organisational unity 2, 4–5, 47–52
  and pension scheme 21–6
  and professional self-government 52–7
  publicity 17–19
  relations with M.P.s 15, 17, 121
  relations with the N.U.T. 4, 48–51, 110
  and the T.U.C. 100–11

Balance of payments 26–7, 37, 43–45, 79

Boyle, Sir Edward 23, 24, 27–9, 30–1
Burnham Committees, The xi, 10, 26–9 *passim*, 41, 62, 64, 64–76 *passim*, 78–9, 95

Campaign For Education 39, 46, 83–6, 88–93, 122
Circulars xi, 6
Central Advisory Councils xi, 11
Conference of Professional and Public Service Organisations (C.O.P.P.S.O.) 94, 95–100, 103, 105, 106
Conservative Party 15–16, 62–3
Council for Educational Advance 39, 46, 86–93
County Councils Association 5
Cripps, Sir Stafford 39
Crosland, Anthony 54, 55, 58, 81–3

Department of Economic Affairs 110
Department of Education
  access to 8–12, 120–1, 127–8
  pressure on 8–12, 20, 21
  relations with local education authorities 5–7, 21–6 *passim*, 31
Department of Education and Science xi
Deputations 10, 11–12, 22, 62
Derby, Lord 8

Eccles, Sir David 22, 26–7, 31, 60, 62, 64, 65, 66, 82
Eckstein, Professor H. vii
Education, demand for 38, 39, 45
Educational administration, system of 5–7, 34–6, 117–18
Educational expenditure
  as a priority 7, 34–6, 37–9, 42, 81–3, 88–9
  cuts in 37, 43–5, 87–8
  growth of 37–9, 44

Gould, Sir Ronald 30, 42, 43, 48, 81, 95, 98, 109
Government structure 5–7, 34–6, 117–18
Granville, Lord 8
Gross National Product 37–9, 45, 81, 89

Headmasters Association (*see also* Joint Four)
  access to the Department of Education 9–12
  and Sir Edward Boyle 27
  and Campaign For Education 83–93 *passim*
  conferences of 23
  and C.O.P.P.S.O. 96
  formation 1, 2
  membership 3
  and militancy 72
  and organisational unity 2, 4–5, 47–52
  and pension schemes 21–6
  and professional self-government 52–7
  publicity 17–19
Headmasters' Conference 1, 9, 12
Hogg, Quintin 54, 63

Incomes Policy 26–9 *passim*, 31, 37, 39–41, 67–8, 71, 73–4, 94, 95–110 *passim*, 105, 109, 119

Jarvis, Fred 84, 125
Joint Four vi, 1, 11, 14, 15, 47–52, 72, 94, 95

Kekewich, Sir George 9

Labour Party 15, 16, 28, 100–1
Lloyd, Selwyn 26–7, 40–1, 95, 97, 98
Local Education Authorities 5–7, 34
Local Education Authority Associations 5–7, 21–6 *passim*, 29–33 *passim*, 69–70, 73, 117–18

Lowe, Sir Robert 8

Memoranda 10, 15
Militancy 41, 46, 59–60, 60–80, 119, 127
Ministry of Education xii
Ministry of Health 34
Morant, Sir Robert 9

National Association of Head Teachers
  and Campaign For Education 83–93 *passim*
  conferences of 23, 25
  formation 2
  and organisational unity 2, 4–5
  and pension schemes 21–6
  and professional self-government 52–7
  publicity 17–19
  relations with M.P.s 14, 15, 16, 121
National Association of Local Government Officers 95, 96, 99, 103, 110
National Asociation of Schoolmasters
  access to the Burnham Committee 10, 15, 62–4, 120
  and Sir Edward Boyle 27
  and Campaign For Education 83–93 *passim*
  conferences of 23, 63, 70, 108
  executive of 102, 124–5
  formation 2
  membership 3, 4, 64
  and militancy 60, 61, 62–4, 71–76, 77, 78
  and organisational unity 2, 4–5, 47–52
  and pension scheme 21–26
  and professional self-government 52–7
  publicity 17–19
  relations with M.P.s 14–17, 121
  relations with the N.U.T. 4, 47–8, 50–1, 52, 62, 70–6 *passim*, 77, 108, 121
  and the T.U.C. 100–11
National Board for Prices and Incomes 40
National Economic Development Council 41–3, 89, 97–9, 105, 106
National economic policy 35, 37, 78
National Federation of Professional Workers 96, 99
National Incomes Commission 40, 97
National Plan, The 42, 89, 109
National Union of Teachers
  access to the Department 9–12
  and Sir Edward Boyle 20, 26–9
  and Campaign For Education 83–93 *passim*
  conferences of 23, 24, 26, 30, 51, 57, 59, 65, 66, 67, 68, 70, 110
  and C.O.P.P.S.O. 94–100
  executive of 26, 51, 66, 67, 68, 72, 77, 101, 102, 124–5
  formation 2
  membership 3, 4
  and militancy 60, 61, 64–76, 77, 78
  and organisational unity 2, 4–5, 47–52, 57–8
  and pension scheme 21–6
  and profesional self-government 52–7
  publicity 17–19
  relations with M.P.s 12–17, 26–39 *passim*, 121
  relations with the N.A.S. 4, 47–8, 50–1, 52, 62, 70–6, *passim*, 77, 108, 121
  and the T.U.C. 100–11
  Young Teachers' conference 59
National Union of Women Teachers 53

Organisational unity 4, 46, 47–52, 57–60 *passim*

Parliament 12–17, 26–9, 29–33 *passim*, 82
Pension schemes 20–6, 29–33 *passim*, 51
Planning 37, 41–3, 94, 99–100, 104–6, 107, 108, 109, 110
Power relationships viii, 30–3, 34–6, 78–9, 81–3, 129
Pressure, traditional forms of 8–33, 58
Professional self-government 46, 52–7, 57–60 *passim*
Public opinion 17–19
Public sector, expenditure in 34–39, 81–93 *passim*
Publicity 17–19

Regulations 6

Schools Council 10–11
Short, Edward 55–6, 57–9
Stewart, Michael 29, 110

Teachers
  degree of unionisation 1, 4
  numbers 1
  occupational distribution 2
  in France 80, 83–4
  in Parliament 16
  in Scotland 23–4, 30

Teachers' Associations
  behaviour of vii, 8, 45–6, 112–114
  determinants of behaviour 32, 33, 36, 39, 40, 43, 45–6, 115–129
  goals, 121–3, 122
  leadership 124–5
  membership 2–5, 123–4
  policy faced 36–45, 118–19
  power relationships faced 30–33, 34–6, 45–6, 81–3, 129
  and politics 83
  unity of 2, 4, 47–52, 52–60 *passim*
Teachers' General Council 45, 53–7, 58, 59, 122
Trades Union Congress (T.U.C.) 40, 41, 46, 94, 96, 98, 100–11, 122, 127
Treasury 34, 35, 40, 45, 81, 82, 112, 118
Tropp, Asher 14

Union of Women Teachers 73

Walker, Patrick Gordon 69, 87
Webb, Beatrice 13
Working Parties 10, 24–5, 30, 54–56, 70